BLACK AMERICANS IN CONGRESS, 1870–1989

A Currier and Ives print of 1872 depicts black members of the Forty-first and Forty-second Congresses. Seated from left to right: Sen. Hiram R. Revels of Mississippi; Rep. Benjamin S. Turner of Alabama; Rep. Josiah T. Walls of Florida; Rep. Joseph H. Rainey of South Carolina; Rep. Robert Brown Elliott of South Carolina. Standing: Rep. Robert C. De Large of South Carolina and Rep. Jefferson F. Long of Georgia. (Library of Congress, Prints and Photographs Division.)

BLACK AMERICANS IN CONGRESS, 1870–1989

By

Bruce A. Ragsdale

and

Joel D. Treese

Office of the Historian,
U.S. House of Representatives
Raymond W. Smock, Historian and Director

U.S. Government Printing Office, Washington, DC, 1990

ENDPAPER

"Electioneering at the South." Wood engraving sketched by W. L. Sheppard from *Harper's Weekly,* July 25, 1868. In the wake of emancipation, blacks throughout the South turned to politics as a means of protecting and advancing their newly-won freedom. This drawing depicts an early political gathering on what appears to be a former plantation. Women join the men in listening to the candidate's appeal. This kind of local political mobilization cultivated a generation of black leadership and prepared the foundation for the election of blacks to Congress.

Library of Congress Cataloging-in-Publication Data

Ragsdale, Bruce A.
  Black Americans in Congress, 1870–1989.

  (House document; no. 101-117)
  Supt. of Docs. no.: Y 1.1/7:101-117
  1. Afro-American legislators—Biography. 2. United States. Congress—Biography. I. Treese, Joel D., 1960–   . II. Title. III. Series: House document (United States. Congress. House);
no. 101-117
E185.96.R25   1990   328.73'92'2   [B]   89-600409

COMMISSION ON THE BICENTENARY OF THE U.S. HOUSE OF REPRESENTATIVES

Lindy (Mrs. Hale) Boggs, *Chairman*

Members

Philip R. Sharp
Thomas M. Foglietta

Bud Shuster
Newt Gingrich
Paul B. Henry

Former Members Serving on Commission

Tom Vandergriff
John J. Rhodes

Ex-Officio Members

Richard A. Gephardt, *Majority Leader*
Robert H. Michel, *Minority Leader*

HOUSE CONCURRENT RESOLUTION 170

One Hundred First Congress, First Session

Submitted by Mrs. Boggs

Resolved by the House of Representatives (the Senate concurring), That the book entitled "Black Americans in Congress" (as revised by the Office for the Bicentennial of the House of Representatives) shall be printed as a House document, with illustrations and suitable binding. In addition to the usual number, 25,000 copies of the book shall be printed for the use of the Office for the Bicentennial of the House of Representatives.

Approved by the House October 23, 1989.
Approved by the Senate November 20, 1989.

Dedicated to the Memory of

Rep. Mickey Leland of Texas

1944–1989

ACKNOWLEDGMENTS

Various offices and individuals provided generous assistance in the preparation of this volume. The staff of the Office of the Historian offers special acknowledgment to: Amelia Parker, Congressional Black Caucus; Clifton H. Johnson and Lester Sullivan, the Amistad Research Center, Tulane University; Mary Ann Ferrarese, Library of Congress; Maricia Battle, Moorland-Spingarn Research Center, Howard University; Kathryn Allamong Jacob and John O. Hamilton, Senate Historical Office; Keith Jewell, Office of Photography, U.S. House of Representatives; the staff of the U.S. House of Representatives Library and the reference staff of the La Follette Reading Room at the Library of Congress.

LETTER OF TRANSMITTAL

The bicentennial year of Congress provides an excellent opportunity to study the rich history of the legislative branch of government during its first two centuries. This new edition of *Black Americans in Congress* will make a significant contribution to understanding that history. The first edition, which was published as part of the congressional observance of the bicentennial of the American Revolution, included an outline of the political careers of the forty-five black men and women who served in Congress between 1870 and 1977. The present volume features expanded biographical essays on those individuals as well as the twenty black Members to win election to the House of Representatives since 1977. The inclusion of bibliographic citations will encourage further reading on these Members of Congress.

The staff of the Office of the Historian prepared this edition as part of its ongoing research on the history of the House of Representatives. The essays describe the varied accomplishments of diverse individuals and collectively illuminate an important dimension of the history of Congress and the nation. The result is a moving story of the black struggle for political equality and opportunity.

The Commission on the Bicentenary of the U.S. House of Representatives is pleased to present this volume as a fitting recognition of black Americans who served in Congress and as a part of the effort to explore further the two-hundred year history of the institution.

Lindy (Mrs. Hale) Boggs
Chairman

Commission on the Bicentenary of the
U.S. House of Representatives

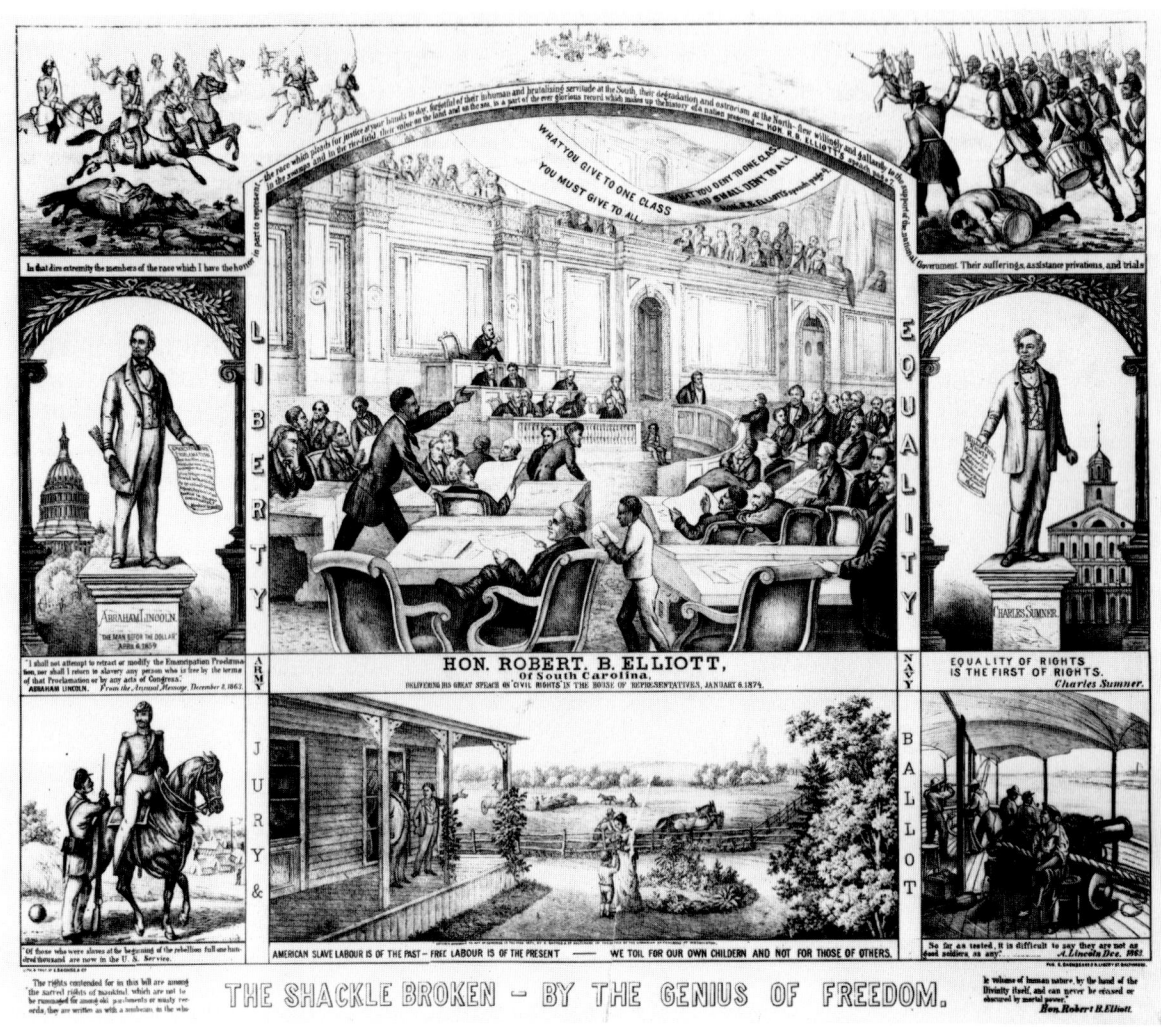

"The Shackle Broken–By the Genius of Freedom," printed in *Frank Leslie's Illustrated Weekly* in 1874, depicts Robert Brown Elliott's celebrated speech of January 6, 1874, in favor of Sen. Charles Sumner's Civil Rights bill. Elliott's speech on the floor of the House of Representatives forms the centerpiece of this celebration of emancipation and the newly-won rights of black Americans. (Library of Congress, Prints and Photographs Division.)

INTRODUCTION

For black Americans the promise of republican government and democratic participation was delayed well beyond the founding of the federal government in 1789. At the time of elections to the First Congress, most blacks lived in slavery and were barred from the political process. State laws denied even free blacks the right of suffrage and excluded them from office holding. For more than seven decades much of the debate and legislation of Congress concerned the status of slavery and directly affected the lives of black Americans, and yet they had no representation in such deliberations. In this bicentennial year of the Congress and the federal government, it is important to recognize that the Constitution we enjoy today evolved over a number of years and did not protect the civil rights of black Americans until after a Civil War and passage of significant amendments.

Only with the enforcement of the Reconstruction Act of 1867 and the ratification of the Fifteenth Amendment did blacks first win seats in Congress. Hiram Revels of Mississippi became the first black to serve in Congress when he took his seat in the Senate on February 25, 1870. Joseph Rainey of South Carolina became the first black Member of the House of Representatives when he took the oath of office on December 12, 1870. Between 1870 and the opening of the One Hundred First Congress sixty-five blacks served in Congress.

Blacks throughout the South became politically active soon after their emancipation and the close of the Civil War. State conventions and local political societies such as the Union League provided an opportunity for freedmen to articulate their vision of full participation in the political and economic life of the former slave states. Out of this broad-based political mobilization emerged a generation of black leadership. Those blacks elected to Congress during Reconstruction found the national legislature an effective forum for the advocacy of political equality. Following the end of federal Reconstruction in 1877, blacks continued to win election to Congress and carried on the struggle for civil rights and economic opportunity. The black representatives of the late-nineteenth century were the most prominent indication of the persistence of political organization on a local level in the South.

The nineteenth-century black congressmen, who unanimously adhered to the Republican Party which had championed the rights of freedmen, often found the struggle for political equality continued after their election. Many of them faced contested elections and spent a good deal of their term defending the legitimacy of their claim to a House seat. Others found it difficult to speak on the floor or were subject to the hostility of various colleagues.

In the 1890s and early 1900s a series of state constitutional conventions and revised election codes effectively disenfranchised most blacks in the South. For nearly three decades no black won election to Congress. During World War I and in the following decade, however, black migration to northern cities established the foundation for political organization in urban centers. Oscar DePriest's election in 1928 as a representative from Chicago began a slow but steady succession of political victories in the North. Over the next three decades blacks won congressional seats in Chicago, New York City, Detroit and Philadelphia. In the wake of the civil rights movement and the enforcement of the Voting Rights Act of 1965 blacks regained seats in the South. In 1972 Barbara Jordan of Texas and Andrew Young of Georgia became the first black representatives elected from the South since George H. White of North Carolina left office in 1901. In the years following the New Deal, all but one black Member, Senator Edward Brooke, have been Democrats.

Since the nineteenth century black Members of Congress have served as advocates for all black Americans as well as representatives for their constituencies. During Reconstruction and the late-nineteenth century black congressmen called on their colleagues to protect the voting rights of blacks and to restrain white vigilante groups in the South. These Members, many of them former slaves, also called for expanded educational opportunities and land grants for freedmen. In the mid-twentieth century black representatives turned to the needs of the urban poor and urged federal programs for improved housing and job training. As the most prominent black officeholders of the time, these representatives served as defenders of the civil rights movement and proponents of legislation to end segregation. In 1971 the establishment of the Congressional Black Caucus offered a formal means of representing the combined interests of black Americans. The Caucus has demonstrated a special concern for the protection of civil rights, the guarantee of equal opportunity in education, employment and housing, and a broad array of issues ranging from United States' policy toward the apartheid government of South Africa to the creation of a federal holiday honoring Dr. Martin Luther King, Jr.

Blacks in Congress have been further united by their shared experience in the African American community. Many of the early black congressmen were born in slavery and nearly all came of age in the racial caste society of the ante-bellum South. The political and economic opportunities of Reconstruction offered these men the hope that blacks might achieve genuine equality in American society while the opposition of many white Southerners reminded them of the need for federal protection of the liberties won in the aftermath of the Civil War.

Until the mid-twentieth century, black Members of Congress like all black Americans, faced the restrictions of legalized segregation. In traveling from their districts they rode on separate train cars, and in Washington, D.C., they confronted segregated theaters, hotels and restaurants. Even the restaurants in the Capitol segregated facilities for white and black staff. Federal office holding offered no exemption from Jim Crow.

Since the victories of the civil rights movement in the 1960s, black men and women have won election to Congress from increasingly diverse regions of the country. Whether from largely urban districts, suburban areas, or more recently from rural Mississippi, these Members have maintained their common concerns with the persistent economic discrepancies between black and white Americans and with the protection of civil rights.

Black Members of Congress also have challenged military and security budgets that deprive domestic social programs of badly-needed funding. These Members have urged a reallocation of spending from the production of nuclear weapons and other defense programs to human services. Through proposals for economic sanctions against nations guilty of human rights violations, such as South Africa, and in plans for emergency food relief in Africa, black representatives have made a collective effort to develop a foreign policy that recognizes the problems of disenfranchised and dispossessed people throughout the world. These concerns were notably, but tragically, exemplified by Rep. Mickey Leland of Texas who, as this volume went to press, was killed in a plane crash while traveling to inspect relief programs at a refugee camp in Ethiopia.

The collected biographies of black Americans who served in the House and Senate provide an important perspective on the history of the Congress and the role of blacks in American politics. During our commemoration of the founding of the nation's government and two-hundred years of the Constitution, these biographies offer eloquent testimony to the long struggle to extend the ideals of the founders to encompass all citizens of the United States.

Ronald V. Dellums, Chair
Congressional Black Caucus

EDWARD WILLIAM BROOKE III

(U.S. Senate Historical Office)

United States Senator
Republican of Massachusetts
Ninetieth—Ninety-fifth Congresses

The only black person ever elected to the Senate by popular vote, Edward Brooke was born in Washington, D.C., on October 26, 1919. He attended the public schools of Washington and graduated with a B.S. from Howard University in 1941. He entered the United States Army as a second lieutenant in 1942 and served in Europe with the 366th Infantry Regiment and with partisans in Italy before his release as a captain in 1945. After receiving an LL.B. from Boston University Law School in 1948 and an LL.M. from the same institution in 1950, he began the practice of law. In 1960 he was the Republican nominee for secretary of the commonwealth, but lost to Kevin H. White. He was chairman of Boston's finance commission from 1961 until 1962, when he was elected attorney general of Massachusetts and served in that office until 1966. On November 8, 1966,

Brooke defeated the Democratic nominee, former governor Endicott Peabody, in the race for the United States Senate.

When Brooke took office on January 3, 1967, he became the first black to serve in the Senate since 1881. During his first term he adhered to liberal and moderate positions that often put him at odds with the Nixon administration. He criticized the White House for neglecting the black community and failing to enforce school integration. Brooke voted against the nominations of Clement F. Haynsworth, Jr., G. Harrold Carswell and William H. Rehnquist to the Supreme Court. A steadfast critic of the administration's Southeast Asian policies, he opposed the invasion of Cambodia and supported the McGovern-Hatfield and Cooper-Church amendments designed to limit American involvement with the war in Vietnam.

In May 1970 Brooke traveled to Jackson State College in Mississippi to help ease tensions resulting from the fatal shootings of two black students by police. In these early days in Congress he demonstrated the strong interest in public housing and mass transit that would characterize his Senate service. He also favored extending minimum wage standards to unprotected jobs held by unskilled workers, providing tax incentives to companies with management training programs, and increasing operating subsidies for commuter rail services and mass transit systems.

Brooke defeated Democrat John J. Droney to win a second Senate term in 1972. In May 1973 he introduced a resolution authorizing the attorney general to appoint a special prosecutor to serve in all criminal investigations arising from the Watergate affair. Six months later Brooke became the first senator to call publicly for Richard Nixon's resignation, asserting that the embattled president no longer possessed the public confidence to govern effectively. In November 1975 he joined seven other Banking Committee colleagues in rejecting President Ford's nomination of former Representative Benjamin B. Blackburn to the Federal Home Loan Bank Board because of his concern about Blackburn's opposition to the 1968 Fair Housing Act.

During the Carter administration Brooke continued to support appropriations for low-income rental housing programs, construction of public housing and the purchase and refurbishment of existing units. He successfully fought against a 1977 amendment to a Health, Education and Welfare bill that would have prevented the department from enforcing quotas to meet affirmative action goals, but he failed to delete an anti-busing clause from an HEW funding measure. Brooke called on the Agency for International Development to establish a minority business section and tried unsuccessfully to prevent the Senate from reducing the American contribution to the United Nations' International Development Association.

Brooke defeated a Republican challenger, Avi Nelson, in the primary of September 1978 only to lose his Senate seat to Fifth District Representative Paul Tsongas in the general election. After leaving office he resumed the practice of law in Washington, D.C.

For further reading:

Becker, John F., and Eugene E. Heaton, Jr. "The Election of Senator Edward W. Brooke." *Public Opinion Quarterly* 31 (Fall 1967): pp. 346–358.

Brooke, Edward W. *The Challenge of Change: Crisis in Our Two-Party System.* Boston: Little, Brown, 1966.

Cutler, John Henry. *Ed Brooke: Biography of a Senator.* Indianapolis: The Bobbs-Merrill Co., Inc., 1972.

Hartshorn, Elinor C. "The Quiet Campaigner: Edward W. Brooke in Massachusetts." Ph.D. dissertation, University of Massachusetts, 1973.

BLANCHE KELSO BRUCE

(U.S. Senate Historical Office)

United States Senator
Republican of Mississippi
Forty-fourth—Forty-sixth Congresses

The first black person to serve a full term in the United States Senate, Blanche K. Bruce was born in slavery near Farmville, Virginia, on March 1, 1841. He was tutored by his master's son and worked as a field hand and printer's apprentice as his master moved him from Virginia to Mississippi and Missouri. Bruce escaped slavery at the opening of the Civil War and attempted to enlist in the Union Army. After the military refused his application, he taught school, briefly attended Oberlin College, and worked as a steamboat porter on the Mississippi River. In 1864 he settled in Hannibal, Missouri, and organized the state's first school for blacks. Five years later he moved to Mississippi where he entered local politics and established himself as a prosperous landowner. In quick succession he was appointed registrar of voters in Tallahatchie County, tax assessor of Bolivar

County, and elected sheriff and tax collector of Bolivar where he also served as supervisor of education. On a trip to the state capital of Jackson in 1870, Bruce gained the attention of powerful white Republicans who dominated Mississippi's Reconstruction government. These men secured more appointments for Bruce and made him the most recognized black political leader in the state. In February 1874, the Mississippi legislature elected Bruce to the United States Senate.

Bruce formally entered the Senate on March 5, 1875, and was elected to three committees: Pensions; Manufactures; and Education and Labor. During the Forty-fifth Congress (1877–79) he served on the Select Committee on the Levee System of the Mississippi River. Although slighted by his Mississippi colleague, James L. Alcorn, Bruce won the friendship and support of Republican senators such as Roscoe Conkling (for whom Bruce would name his only child), and enjoyed a more amicable relationship with Alcorn's Democratic successor, Lucius Q.C. Lamar. Bruce made repeated though futile attempts to convince his fellow senators to seat Louisiana's former governor and black political leader, P.B.S. Pinchback. He encouraged the government to be more generous in issuing western land grants to black emigrants and favored distribution of duty-free clothing from England to needy blacks who had emigrated to Kansas from the South. Bruce also appealed for the desegregation of United States Army units and for a Senate inquiry into the violent Mississippi elections of 1875. As a member and temporary chairman of the Committee on River Improvements, he advocated the development of a channel and levee system and construction of the Mississippi Valley and Ship Island Railroad.

On February 14, 1879, during debate on a Chinese exclusion bill that he opposed, Bruce became the first black senator to preside over a Senate session. In April he was appointed chairman of the Select Committee to Investigate the Freedman's Savings and Trust Company. Bruce's six-member committee issued a report naming bank officials who were guilty of fraud and incompetence. Eventually about 61,000 depositors victimized by the bank's 1874 failure received a portion of their money. In January 1880 the Mississippi legislature, now controlled by Democrats, chose James Z. George to succeed Bruce. Before his term ended the following March, Bruce continued to be an activist senator, calling for a more equitable and humane Indian policy and demanding a War Department investigation of the brutal harassment of a black West Point cadet. At the 1880 Republican convention in Chicago, Bruce served briefly as presiding officer and received eight votes for vice president.

Following the close of his Senate service on March 3, 1881, Bruce rejected an offer of the ministry to Brazil because slavery was still practiced there. All but one member of the Mississippi congressional delegation endorsed Bruce for a seat in President Garfield's cabinet, but he instead received appointment as registrar of the treasury and served until the Democrats regained power in 1885. Bruce became a lecturer, an author of magazine articles, and was superintendent of the exhibit on black achievement at the World's Cotton Exposition in New Orleans during 1884–1885. In 1888 Bruce received eleven votes for vice president at the convention that nominated Benjamin Harrison. Harrison, as president, appointed Bruce recorder of deeds for the District of Columbia in 1889. After leaving this office in 1893 Bruce was a trustee of public schools in Washington, D.C., and again registrar of the treasury from 1897 until his death in Washington on March 17, 1898.

For further reading:

Drake, Sadie D. St. Clair. "The National Career of Blanche Kelso Bruce." Ph.D. dissertation, New York University, 1947.

Harris, William C. "Blanche K. Bruce of Mississippi: Conservative Assimilationist." In *Southern Black Leaders of the Reconstruction Era,* edited by Howard N. Rabinowitz, pp. 3-38. Urbana: University of Illinois Press, 1982.

Mann, Kenneth E. "Blanche Kelso Bruce: United States Senator without a Constituency." *Journal of Mississippi History* 38 (May 1976): pp. 183-198.

Shapiro, Samuel L. "A Black Senator from Mississippi: Blanche K. Bruce (1841-1898)." *Review of Politics* 44 (January 1982): pp. 83-109.

YVONNE BRATHWAITE BURKE

(U.S. House of Representatives)

United States Representative
Democrat of California
Ninety-third—Ninety-fifth Congresses

Yvonne Burke was born Perle Yvonne Watson in Los Angeles on October 5, 1932. After attending public schools in her native city, she received a B.A. in political science from the University of California-Los Angeles in 1953 and a J.D. from the University of Southern California School of Law in 1956. She commenced practice in Los Angeles the same year she graduated from law school. She was California's deputy corporation commissioner, a hearing officer for the Los Angeles Police Commission, and an attorney on the staff of the McCone Commission which investigated the causes of the Watts riots of 1965. In 1966 she became the first black woman elected to the California state assembly and served until 1972 when she defeated Republican candidate Gregg Tria to win election as a United States Representative from California's Thirty-seventh District.

During her first term in the House Burke was a member of the Committee on Interior and Insular Affairs and the Public Works Committee. In December 1974 she joined the Committee on Appropriations. As a member of that influential committee, Burke proposed an amendment to a Community Services Administration bill which called for additional funding of community food and nutrition programs and other services for senior citizens, but it was rejected by the full House. When a majority of the Appropriations Committee recommended censure of nations that requested American aid while voting against United States interests at the United Nations, Burke joined Representative Louis Stokes of Ohio in dissent. Concerned about the unemployment rate in the nation and particularly in the Twenty-eighth District, which had been hurt by layoffs in the aerospace, automobile and electronics industries, she supported the Humphrey-Hawkins bill creating a federally-coordinated program of full employment. Burke called on President Ford to match federal plans to resettle Vietnamese refugees with programs to relieve poverty and unemployment.

In January 1976 the Congressional Black Caucus unanimously chose Burke as its first woman chair. Five months later she joined four other caucus members in an effort to persuade Attorney General Edward Levi not to file a brief with the Supreme Court in behalf of opponents of a Boston school busing plan. In June of 1977, she helped salvage a $50 million American donation to countries in Africa's Sahel region fighting a large-scale drought. Burke repeatedly sought to restrict foreign aid to nations guilty of human rights violations.

After Vernon E. Jordan, executive director of the National Urban League, criticized President Carter's record on civil rights and social programs, Burke and other caucus members endorsed his statement and warned Carter that his support among black Americans was diminishing. She tried to restore the Housing and Urban Development Department's planning grant funds for use in urban areas. On January 4, 1977, she introduced the Displaced Homemakers Act, which authorized the Department of Health, Education and Welfare, to establish at least fifty job financial training and counseling centers for women new to the labor market and lacking in job skills.

In 1978 Burke chose to run for state attorney general of California rather than seek re-election to the House. After her defeat in that election, Governor Edmund G. Brown, Jr., appointed her to the Los Angeles County Board of Supervisors where she served from June 1979 until her resignation in December 1980. She continues to practice law in Los Angeles.

RICHARD HARVEY CAIN

(W.H. Barnes, *The American Government.* Washington, 1875)

United States Representative
Republican of South Carolina
Forty-third—Forty-fifth Congresses

Richard Harvey Cain was one of the leaders of Reconstruction-era Charleston and the first black clergyman to serve in the House of Representatives. He was born to free parents in Greenbrier County, Virginia, on April 12, 1825. He moved with his parents to Gallipolis, Ohio, in 1831 and attended school while working on steamboats along the Ohio River. Cain entered the ministry of the Methodist Episcopal Church in Hannibal, Missouri, in 1844, but was unhappy with the segregation practiced within the denomination and in 1848 joined the African Methodist Episcopal Church. He was a pastor in Muscatine, Iowa, and studied for a year at Wilberforce University before moving to Brooklyn, New York, in 1861. In 1865, the A.M.E. Church sent Cain to South Carolina where he revived the fortunes of Charleston's historic Emmanuel Church and established churches throughout the state. Cain was a delegate to the state constitutional convention of 1868 and a member of the state senate from 1868 to 1870. At the same time he tried to encourage the growth of black-owned and operated farms by purchasing extensive tracts of land for sale to freedmen. From 1866 to 1872 he was editor and publisher of the *South Carolina Leader* (renamed the *Missionary Record* in April 1868); future Representative Robert B. Elliott worked as his associate editor.

In 1872 Cain was elected to an at-large seat in the House of Representatives, defeating Lewis E. Johnson, who ran as an Independent Democrat. As a member of the Forty-third Congress, he took a seat on the Committee on Agriculture. He joined several of his fellow black representatives in advocating passage of the civil rights bill originally introduced by Senator Charles Sumner in 1870. In a speech supporting this bill to desegregate juries, public transportation and accommodations, and schools, Cain described his own experiences with racial discrimination during his train trip to Washington. He declined to seek renomination after his at-large seat was eliminated in 1874 although he remained active in efforts to reform South Carolina's Republican Party after he returned to his ministry. In 1876 he was elected to Congress from the Second District over the Democratic candidate, Michael P. O'Connor. Although O'Connor charged that election irregularities invalidated Cain's claim to the seat, the House twice voted in Cain's favor. He was sworn in to the Forty-fifth Congress on March 4, 1877, and served on the Committee on Private Claims.

In March 1878 Cain, a strong supporter of compulsory public schooling since his days in the South Carolina legislature, introduced a bill requiring the federal government to set aside proceeds from public land sales in an educational fund to be apportioned among the states according to population. He denied that poor education was largely confined to southern blacks and offered statistics to demonstrate the pattern of illiteracy and poor school attendance among southern whites as well. Cain's proposal for the establishment of a mail and passenger shipline between ports in the United States and Liberia reflected his support of opportunities for emigration by blacks in the post-Reconstruction South. He was active in the affairs of the Liberian Exodus Joint Stock Steamship Company, founded in 1877 to encourage the African emigration movement. Cain failed to gain renomination in 1878 as Republicans turned instead to former Representative Edmund W. M. Mackey, who lost the election to O'Connor.

In 1880 Cain was elected a bishop of the African Methodist Episcopal Church and served the Texas-Louisiana conference. He helped establish Paul Quinn College in Waco and served as its president until July 1884. Cain returned to Washington in that year to preside as bishop of the New Jersey Conference, a district covering New England, New Jersey, New York and Philadelphia. He died in Washington on January 18, 1887.

For further reading:

Lewis, Ronald L. "Cultural Pluralism and Black Reconstruction: The Public Career of Richard H. Cain." *The Crisis* 85 (February 1987): pp. 57-60, pp. 64-65.

Mann, Kenneth Eugene. "Richard Harvey Cain, Congressman, Minister and Champion for Civil Rights." *Negro History Bulletin* 35 (March 1972): pp. 64-66.

HENRY PLUMMER CHEATHAM

(Moorland-Spingarn Research Center, Howard University)

United States Representative
Republican of North Carolina
Fifty-first—Fifty-second Congresses

An experienced educator, Henry Plummer Cheatham spent much of his congressional career supporting efforts to teach nineteenth-century Americans about the contributions and achievements of their black fellow citizens. Cheatham was born a slave near Henderson in Granville (now Vance) County, North Carolina, on December 27, 1857. He attended a Henderson public school and entered the normal school of Shaw University in Raleigh in 1875. In 1878 he entered the University's college department, receiving an A.B. degree in 1882. From 1883 to 1884 Cheatham served as principal of the Plymouth Normal School while his wife, Louise Cherry Cheatham, taught instrumental music at the school. Cheatham returned to Henderson and was elected to two terms as register of deeds of Vance County, serving from 1884 to 1888. In 1887 he received an honorary M.A. degree

15

from Shaw University and in the same year was one of the founders and incorporators of an orphanage for black children at Oxford, North Carolina. At the same time he studied law but was unable to practice because of his time-consuming work as recorder of deeds.

In 1888 he was elected as a Republican to the Fifty-first Congress, edging the incumbent, Furnifold McL. Simmons, by 653 votes out of over 32,000 cast. Cheatham became a member of the Committee on Education and the Committee on Expenditures on Public Buildings. He attempted to acquire funds for the erection of a public building at Henderson and asked that money be set aside for additional relief for Robert Smalls and the crew of the steamer *Planter,* who had performed heroic service for the federal government during the Civil War. Like other black representatives of the period, he introduced a bill to reimburse the 61,000 depositors of the Freedman's Savings and Trust Company for losses incurred by its failure in 1874. None of Cheatham's proposals were enacted, and he reintroduced the bills for relief of Freedman's Bank depositors and the *Planter* crew during the next Congress, with equally unsuccessful results. He also presented legislation calling on the federal government to establish and provide temporary support for common schools in the United States.

Cheatham won reelection in 1890 over Democrat James M. Mewborne. Due to the defeats of John Mercer Langston and Thomas E. Miller in the 1890 elections, Cheatham was the only black member of the Fifty-second Congress. He became a member of the Committee on Agriculture in addition to his other committee assignments. Although the illness of Louise Cheatham and his own poor health often prevented him from attending sessions, he was a clear advocate of legislation to inform the nation of the contributions black citizens had made to American life since Emancipation. In May 1892 he asked Congress to appropriate $100,000 for an exhibit of black arts, crafts, tools, and industrial and agricultural products as part of the United States Government exhibit at the World's Columbian Exposition, scheduled to open in Chicago in October. Both political parties, Cheatham said, needed to recognize what black Americans had accomplished in the generation following slavery. He was also interested in securing funding for the appointment of a biracial panel to conduct and publish a census of the educational, financial and social progress of black Americans. In July he asked that there be placed in the adjutant general's office an exhibit of documents on the history of United States military service by blacks in peace and war. The House, however, failed to adopt Cheatham's various proposals.

In his bid for reelection in 1892, Cheatham faced dissent from fellow Republicans and the new Populist Party. He lost the seat to Democrat Frederick A. Woodard. Two years later he made another bid for the seat, only to lose the nomination to his brother-in-law, George H. White. (White, elected, would serve two terms in Congress). Cheatham returned in 1897 to Washington, D.C., where President McKinley appointed him recorder of deeds for the District of Columbia. Following his confirmation by the Senate, Cheatham worked at his post for four years. In 1907 he became superintendent of the Oxford orphanage he helped found two decades earlier and over the next twenty-eight years expanded its facilities and farm land. By the time of his death it housed almost 200 students. Cheatham also served as president of the Negro Association of North Carolina. He died at Oxford on November 29, 1935.

For further reading:

Reid, George W. "Four In Black: North Carolina's Black Congressmen, 1874-1901." *Journal of Negro History* 64 (Summer 1979): pp. 229-243.

SHIRLEY ANITA CHISHOLM

(U.S. House of Representatives)

United States Representative
Democrat of New York
Ninety-first—Ninety-seventh Congresses

Shirley Chisholm, the first black woman elected to Congress, was born Shirley Anita St. Hill on November 30, 1924, in Brooklyn. As a young girl she lived with her grandparents in Barbados, where she attended the Vauxhall Coeducational School. After six years she returned to Brooklyn and attended the public schools. She graduated from Brooklyn College in 1946 with a B.A. in sociology. In 1952 she received an M.A. from Columbia University. She worked as a nursery school teacher at the Mount Calvary Child Care Center in New York from 1946 until 1952, when she became nursery school director at the Friend in Need Nursery in Brooklyn. From 1953 until 1959 she was director of New York's Hamilton-Madison Child Care Center before becoming an educational consultant for New York's Division of Day Care. In 1964 she was elected to the state assembly from the

17

Fifty-fifth district, serving until 1968. In 1968 she defeated civil rights leader James Farmer, who ran on the Republican and Liberal Party tickets, and Conservative Party candidate Ralph J. Carrano to win election to the House from New York's Twelfth District.

Shortly after her arrival in Congress, Chisholm, an outspoken opponent of the seniority system, was assigned by Democratic members of the Ways and Means Committee to the Committee on Agriculture and its Rural Development and Forestry Subcommittee. Before a party caucus, she protested the assignment as inappropriate for the representative of an inner-city district. She soon transferred to a seat on the Veterans' Affairs Committee. Chisholm also served on the Rules Committee and the Education and Labor Committee during her seven terms in the House. In March 1970 she was appointed to the Committee on Organization Study and Review, which recommended reforms in the selection of committee chairs. House Democrats approved the panel's suggestions in January 1971.

Early in her first term Chisholm joined a bipartisan coalition of fifteen representatives introducing legislation to end the draft and create an all-volunteer force. As a member of a House consumer affairs study group, she co-sponsored a measure to establish a national commission on consumer protection and product safety. She worked for the repeal of section two of the Internal Security Act of 1950, which required suspected subversives to be interned in emergency detention camps (the House voted to rescind the law in September 1971). She called for an end to British arms sales to South Africa and to discrimination in the hiring practices of food store chains and automobile manufacturers. An early proponent of increased day care programs, Chisholm proposed funding increases to extend the hours of child care facilities and expand such services to include the working mothers of both middle class and low-income families. She also co-sponsored the Adequate Income Act of 1971, guaranteeing an annual income to families.

On January 25, 1972, Chisholm declared her candidacy for the Democratic presidential nomination. She campaigned extensively and entered primaries in twelve states, winning twenty-eight delegates and receiving 152 first ballot votes at the convention. The following year she attacked the Nixon administration's plan to eliminate the Office of Economic Opportunity and played a leading role in the drive to expand the coverage of minimum wage legislation to include domestic workers. She gathered support from organized labor and the women's movement and on the House floor delivered an impassioned speech recalling the hardships of her own mother's work as a domestic.

In 1976 Chisholm urged the House to override President Ford's veto of a $125 million bill to assist states in meeting federal health, safety and personnel standards for day care centers, and fought to toughen fair housing legislation. Concerned about a possible weakening of special programs for minority students, she opposed creation of the Department of Education and also took a stand against tax credits to defray tuition to private schools, arguing that such credits would undermine the school system. During the Reagan administration she spoke out against cuts in federal block grants for local education agencies.

Chisholm declined to run for reelection in 1982, citing the difficulties of effecting change in an increasingly conservative political atmosphere and her desire to return to private life. She lives in Williamsville, N.Y.

For further reading:

Chisholm, Shirley. *The Good Fight*. New York: Harper and Row, 1973.

_____. *Unbought and Unbossed*. Boston: Houghton Mifflin Co., 1970.

WILLIAM LACY CLAY

(Office of Representative Clay)

United States Representative
Democrat of Missouri
Ninety-first—One Hundred First Congresses

A native of St. Louis, William Lacy Clay has represented the First District of Missouri since his election in 1968. Clay was born in St. Louis on April 30, 1931, and graduated from St. Louis University with a B.S. in history and political science in 1953. Soon after his return from military service, he became involved in local politics and civil rights activity in St. Louis. He also worked as a real estate broker and manager with a life insurance company.

Clay won his first elective office as an alderman from St. Louis' Twenty-sixth Ward in 1959. He held that position until 1964 when he became a committeeman from the same ward. Clay's early political career coincided with his activity as a union official. He was a business representative for the city employee's union from 1961 to 1964 and education coordinator with a local steamfitters' union in 1966 and 1967.

In 1968 Clay entered the Democratic primary for the open seat in the First District. He defeated four candidates for the nomination and went on to win easily the general election. As a member of the House of Representatives he has focused on the same kind of issues that originally attracted him to political office. He serves on the Committee on Education and Labor, where he is chairman of the Subcommittee on Labor-Management Relations. He also serves on the Committee on House Administration and is chairman of the Subcommittee on Libraries and Memorials. He is ranking member on the Post Office and Civil Service Committee. He is a member of the Congressional Black Caucus of which he was a founder in 1971.

Clay was the House sponsor of revisions in the pension law that were incorporated in the Tax Reform Act of 1986. He also has used his committee seats to sponsor legislation for parental and medical leave, for mandatory notification of plant closings, and for the protection of unions' negotiating rights.

CARDISS COLLINS

(Office of Representative Collins)

United States Representative
Democrat of Illinois
Ninety-third—One Hundred First Congresses

Cardiss Collins entered the Ninety-third Congress after winning a special election to fill the vacancy left by the death of her husband. She soon established herself as an effective representative in her own right and has won reelection to the eight succeeding Congresses. Throughout her congressional career she has taken special interest in the social and economic issues important to her district on Chicago's West Side.

Collins was born Cardiss H. Robertson in St. Louis, Missouri, on September 24, 1931, and moved to Detroit at the age of ten. After graduating from the Detroit High School of Commerce, she moved to Chicago to attend Northwestern University. Collins began work as a secretary for the Illinois Department of Labor and soon thereafter for the Illinois Department of Revenue. She worked with the

Department of Revenue as an auditor until her election to Congress.

A keen interest in politics led Collins into involvement with the Chicago Democratic establishment, and she became committeewoman of the city's Twenty-fourth Ward Regular Democratic Organization. She was actively involved in her husband's campaigns as alderman, committeeman and congressman. After George Collins died in a plane crash near Chicago's Midway Airport in 1972, Cardiss Collins handily won the special election to fill his seat on June 5, 1973.

Since her first term in Congress, she has served on the Government Operations Committee, where she was chair of the Subcommittee on Manpower and Housing and now holds the chair of the Subcommittee on Government Activities and Transportation. In this position Collins has gained national attention for her investigations of airport security and advocacy of air safety issues. She also served on the Committee on International Relations (later Foreign Affairs) and since 1981 has sat on the Energy and Commerce Committee. She is a member of the Select Committee on Narcotics Abuse and Control. As a Democratic whip-at-large, she is both the first black and the first woman to hold such a position. In addition to her political career, Collins is an active member of various civic organizations.

GEORGE WASHINGTON COLLINS

(Congressional Black Caucus)

United States Representative
Democrat of Illinois
Ninety-first—Ninety-second Congresses

George Washington Collins was born in Chicago on March 5, 1925. After graduating from Waller High School he entered the United States Army as a private in 1943, serving with the Engineers in the South Pacific before his discharge as a sergeant in 1946. Collins graduated from Central Y.M.C.A. College in 1954 and was a clerk with the Chicago Municipal Court while earning a business law degree from Northwestern University in 1957.

From 1958 to 1961 he was deputy sheriff of Cook County and served as secretary to Alderman Benjamin Lewis of the Twenty-fourth Ward, and as an administrative assistant to the Chicago Board of Health. After Lewis' death in 1963 Collins succeeded him as Twenty-fourth Ward alderman and remained in that office until his election to Congress.

When Sixth District Representative Daniel J. Ronan died in August 1969, Collins was elected to fill out Ronan's unexpired term in the Ninety-first Congress and for a full term in the Ninety-second Congress. He began his service on November 3, 1970, and was a member of the Public Works and Government Operations Committees. Collins supported, in principle, the Nixon administration's proposals to provide a minimum federal payment to low-income families with children and to share federal tax revenues with states and localities, but criticized the plans' funding levels as inadequate. He sought to increase funding for the Elementary and Secondary Education Act and advocated passage of federal highway legislation that addressed the needs of mass transit programs and of urban residents removed from their neighborhoods by road construction. Collins also introduced a bill requiring the Treasury Department to provide free tax preparation service to low- and moderate-income taxpayers. He joined in efforts to reform the Federal Housing Administration after hearings conducted by the Government Operations' Subcommittee on Legal and Monetary Affairs revealed that low-income homeowners had been defrauded by speculators, real estate brokers and home repair companies.

On December 8, 1972, a month after his reelection to a second term, Collins was killed in an airplane crash while traveling to Chicago to help purchase toys for the Twenty-fourth Ward's annual children's Christmas party.

JOHN CONYERS, Jr.

(Office of Representative Conyers)

United States Representative
Democrat of Michigan
Eighty-ninth—One Hundred First Congresses

Now serving his twelfth term in the House of Representatives, John Conyers has focused his legislative efforts on some of the most notable social and economic issues of his time. He was born May 16, 1929, in Detroit, where he attended the public schools and graduated from Northwestern High School in 1947. He worked in an automobile factory and as director of education for United Auto Workers Local 900 before enlisting in 1950 in the United States Army. He was commissioned a second lieutenant in the Corps of Engineers and saw combat action in Korea before his discharge in 1954.

Conyers received a B.A. degree from Wayne State University in 1957 and a LL.B. degree from Wayne State School of Law in 1959. Admitted to the bar in 1959, he began practice in Detroit, worked as a legislative assistant to Representative John J. Dingell, Jr., from 1958 to 1961 and as a referee for the Michigan Workmen's Compensation Department from 1961 to 1963. Conyers was active in the civil rights movement as one of the founders and a member of the National Lawyers Committee for Civil Rights Under Law, and served as general counsel for the Detroit Trade Union Leadership Council.

In 1964 Conyers was elected to the House from Michigan's First Congressional District. An early opponent of the Vietnam War, he helped introduce home rule and congressional representation legislation for Washington, D.C., supported lowering the voting age to eighteen and called for the abolition of the House Committee on Un-American Activities. He is currently a senior member of the Judiciary Committee and chairs its Criminal Justice Subcommittee, where he has presided over hearings on criminal justice issues such as police violence, white collar crime, grand jury reform and revisions in the nation's criminal code.

A long-time foe of capital punishment, Conyers supports the anti-fraud provisions of the civil Racketeer-Influenced and Corrupt Organizations law and has successfully sponsored legislation to provide inmates of correctional institutions with literacy and vocational training. The chairman of the Government Operations Committee, beginning in the 101st Congress, Conyers also serves on the Small Business Committee, the Speaker's Task Force on Minority Set-asides, and was a founder of the Congressional Black Caucus. He is the author of nuclear freeze and anti-apartheid legislation and was a principal sponsor of the Voting Rights Act of 1965, the 1978 Humphrey-Hawkins Full Employment Act and the 1983 Martin Luther King, Jr., holiday bill.

GEORGE WILLIAM CROCKETT, Jr.

(Office of Representative Crockett)

United States Representative
Democrat of Michigan
Ninety-sixth—One Hundred First Congresses

George Crockett entered Congress in 1980 after a lengthy career as a lawyer and judge. Born in Jacksonville, Florida, on August 10, 1909, Crockett attended public schools in his native city and graduated with an A.B. from Morehouse College in Atlanta in 1931. He went north to study law at the University of Michigan where he received his J.D. in 1934.

Crockett returned to Jacksonville to begin his practice of law. His involvement with labor law took him to Washington in 1939 as the first black lawyer with the U.S. Department of Labor. In 1943 President Roosevelt appointed Crockett a hearing examiner with the newly-formed Fair Employment Practices Commission. A year later, he moved to Detroit to become director of a fair employment practices office with the United Auto Workers.

After his return to private practice in 1946, Crockett remained active in the defense of labor unions and civil rights organizers. He represented clients before the House Un-American Activities Committee and the U.S. Supreme Court. He served as judge of the Recorders Court in Detroit from 1966 to 1978 and in 1974 was elected presiding judge of that court. He also served as a visiting judge on the Michigan Court of Appeals and as corporation counsel for the City of Detroit.

Crockett was a well-known leader in Detroit's black community when he declared his candidacy for the congressional seat left vacant by the resignation of Charles Diggs in 1980. He was elected to fill that vacancy on November 4, 1980, and at the same time was elected for the full term of the Ninety-seventh Congress. He was sworn in on November 12, 1980.

In 1987 and 1988 Crockett served as a member of the United States delegation to the forty-second General Assembly of the United Nations. He previously was a member of the U.S. congressional delegation to the International Parliamentary meeting in Havana in 1981 and the Seventh U.N. Congress on Prevention of Crime meeting in Milan, Italy, in 1984.

In the House of Representatives, Crockett serves as a member of the Committee on Foreign Affairs, the Committee on the Judiciary, and the Select Committee on Aging. At the opening of the One Hundredth Congress, he became chairman of the Foreign Affairs Subcommittee on Western Hemisphere Affairs which oversees United States policy in Latin America and the Caribbean. Crockett also has used his seat on Foreign Affairs to voice his opposition to the South African government's policy of apartheid.

WILLIAM LEVI DAWSON

(Library of Congress)

United States Representative
Democrat of Illinois
Seventy-eighth—Ninety-first Congresses

William Levi Dawson was born in Albany, Dougherty County, Georgia, on April 26, 1886, the son of Levi Dawson, a barber, and his wife, the former Rebecca Kendrick. After graduating from Albany Normal School in 1905, Dawson worked as a porter and waiter to earn his way through Fisk University, where he graduated in 1909. Three years later he moved to Chicago and attended the Kent College of Law and Northwestern University. In 1917 he became a first lieutenant with the 365th Infantry of the American Expeditionary Force and was wounded during service in Europe. After returning to Chicago he graduated from Northwestern and was admitted to the bar in 1920.

Dawson entered Chicago politics as a Republican precinct captain and met with mixed success, losing a 1928 congressional primary race but succeeding in 1933 in election to the city council, where he served for six years. He was nominated for the House from the First Congressional District in 1938 but was beaten by Arthur W. Mitchell and the next year failed in his bid for reelection to the city council.

The turning point in Dawson's political life came in 1939 when he accepted Mayor Edward J. Kelly's offer of the post of Democratic committeeman for the Second Ward. Dawson organized his base there thoroughly and sent his precinct workers to organize other predominantly black wards into Democratic voting blocs. In time Dawson's followers controlled as many as five wards that generally offered overwhelming majorities to local, state, and national Democratic candidates. When Mitchell relinquished his House seat in 1942, Dawson won the nomination and defeated his Republican opponent, William E. King, to begin a twenty-seven year congressional career.

In many respects Dawson was an atypical politician and machine leader. He disliked personal publicity, regarded the media with wariness and lived in an unpretentious manner. When in his district Dawson spent part of each day at his headquarters listening to complaints, requests and opinions from a parade of constituents. He kept a tight grip on his share of power in Chicago, dispensing patronage and favors through his political machine and its ancillary organizations. Dawson was also an important figure in the upper echelons of the Chicago Democratic machine (he played a key role in the slating of Richard J. Daley for mayor in 1955), and the national Democratic Party. In 1960 President-elect Kennedy, whose narrow victory in Illinois owed much to voters in Dawson's wards, asked him to join the cabinet as postmaster general. The seventy-four year old Dawson declined and indicated that he would be of more help to the new administration by remaining in the House.

In 1949 Dawson became the first black representative to chair a major committee when he assumed control of the Committee on Expenditures in Executive Departments (renamed the Committee on Government Operations in 1952), a position he retained, with a two-year hiatus, until his death. Dawson rarely missed the chance to cast votes favorable to civil rights measures. He sought better appointments for blacks in the federal civil service and judiciary, supported southern voter registration drives and blocked congressional efforts to discredit the integration of public schools in Washington, D.C. He also opposed poll taxes and legislation that he thought placed too much of a tax burden on low-income citizens. In 1951 Dawson helped defeat the Winstead amendment, which would have permitted military personnel to choose whether they wanted to serve in white or black units. As his power in Washington grew, however, Dawson came under increasing attack from critics who contended that he was more loyal to the city and national Democratic Party than to the cause of civil rights. Some of Dawson's own staffers were disappointed by his opposition to the anti-discriminatory Powell Amendment. (Dawson disliked the amendment because he feared that as part of appropriations bills it would jeopardize all federal aid to education.) Unlike his contemporary, Adam Clayton Powell, Dawson offered little specific legislation to advance the drive for black equality.

By the mid-1960s Dawson's organization exhibited signs of decay. Burdened by age and ill health, he skillfully allowed himself to recede into the background while gradually promoting chosen lieutenants. On November 9, 1970, six days after his hand-picked successor, Ralph H. Metcalfe, was elected to his seat, Dawson died in Chicago.

For further reading:

Wilson, James Q. "Two Negro Politicians: An Interpretation." *Midwest Journal of Political Science* 4 (November 1960): pp. 346–369.

ROBERT CARLOS DE LARGE

(Library of Congress)

United States Representative
Republican of South Carolina
Forty-second Congress

The brief congressional career of Robert Carlos De Large was largely overshadowed by a prolonged challenge to his election. De Large was born a slave in Aiken, South Carolina, on March 15, 1842. He managed to acquire as much of an education as he could at the Wood High School in Charleston. He later worked as a farmer, tailor and Freedman's Bureau agent before becoming an organizer for South Carolina's Republican Party. He chaired the credentials committee at the 1865 Colored People's Convention held in Charleston's Zion Church and the platform committee of the 1867 Republican State Convention. He served on the Committee on Franchise and Elections at the 1868 South Carolina Constitutional Convention. In the same year he was elected to the state house of representatives and became chairman of its ways and means committee. In 1870 the legislature appointed him land commissioner to oversee the sale and transfer of almost two thousand small tracts of land to homeowners who would pay for them over a maximum of eight years.

De Large was in the land commissioner's post when he was nominated for Congress from the Second Congressional District. On October 19, 1870, he defeated another Republican candidate, Christopher C. Bowen, by 986 votes out of over 32,000 cast. Bowen promptly challenged the result, but this did not prevent De Large from being sworn into the Forty-second Congress when it convened on March 4, 1871. He was assigned to the Committee on Manufactures

During the first session, De Large offered an amendment to a deficiency appropriation bill to provide $20,000 to rebuild a Charleston orphan asylum maintained by nuns who had cared for Union troops during the bombardment of Charleston. When the House debated an act to remove political restrictions from former Confederates, De Large thought it more important to provide loyal southerners federal protection from intimidation and terror.

In April the House considered a measure to enforce the Fourteenth Amendment. De Large told the House that although no persecution of freedmen had taken place in his own district, intolerable conditions elsewhere in the South required that Congress take action to curb white supremacy groups. Replying to New York's Democratic Representative Samuel S. Cox, who charged that South Carolina's blacks had been collectively responsible for permitting corruption to flourish in the state government, De Large maintained that blacks were guilty only of placing too much faith in untrustworthy carpetbaggers.

The House Committee on Elections began consideration of Christopher Bowen's claim in December 1871, and De Large, despite failing health, took a leave of absence the following April to prepare a case defending himself. On January 18, 1873, the committee reported that so many abuses and irregularities had taken place during the election that it was unable to determine who had received a majority of the votes legally cast. The committee decided that neither De Large nor Bowen was entitled to the seat and declared it vacant. In 1872 De Large had declined to run for reelection and another black South Carolinian, Alonzo J. Ransier, succeeded him.

De Large lived in the state capital, Columbia, for a time but returned to Charleston after Republican governor Robert K. Scott appointed him a magistrate in that city. At his residence on Calhoun Street the thirty-one year old De Large died of consumption on February 14, 1874.

RONALD V. DELLUMS

(Office of Representative Dellums)

United States Representative
Democrat of California
Ninety-second—One Hundred First Congresses

Ronald Dellums attracted national attention in his first campaign for the House of Representatives in 1970. Coretta Scott King campaigned for him, and Vice President Spiro Agnew visited the district in an effort to defeat this vocal critic of the Nixon administration's policy in Vietnam. In the Democratic primary that year, Dellums defeated six-term incumbent Jeffrey Cohelan and went on to win the general election in the district that includes Berkeley and Oakland. Throughout his congressional career he has continued to attract broad attention on a number of issues.

Dellums was born the son of a longshoreman and labor organizer in Oakland, California, on November 24, 1935. After serving two years in the Marine Corps, he enrolled at San Francisco State College where he received a B.A. in 1960. Two years later he earned a masters degree in social welfare from the University of California at Berkeley.

A career as a psychiatric social worker in Berkeley led to Dellums' involvement with community affairs and local politics. He won a seat on the Berkeley City Council in 1967 and emerged as a spokesman for minorities and the disadvantaged. From his seat on the council, Dellums mounted his campaign for the House in 1970. As a Member of Congress he continued to focus on the social issues that concerned him in Berkeley and established himself as a forceful opponent of a growing defense budget. During his first term in the House, he held ad hoc hearings on military policy in Vietnam and racism in the armed services. Beginning in 1973, he pursued his interest in the American military from his seat on the Armed Services Committee. He became chairman of the Subcommittee on Military Installations and Facilities in 1983. Since 1979 he has chaired the Committee on the District of Columbia.

During his tenure in the House of Representatives, Dellums has introduced legislation on a wide variety of issues including comprehensive health care, housing, the environment, youth employment, and restrictions on nuclear arms deployment. He repeatedly sponsored measures to end United States support for the government of South Africa. The Congressional Black Caucus recognized Dellums' leadership on these and other issues by electing him chair of the caucus in December 1988.

For further reading:

James, Victor Vernon, Jr. "Cultural Pluralism and the Quest for Black Citizenship: The 1970 Ronald V. Dellums Congressional Primary Campaign." Ph.D. dissertation, University of California, Berkeley, 1975.

OSCAR STANTON DE PRIEST

(Library of Congress)

United States Representative
Republican of Illinois
Seventy-first—Seventy-third Congresses

Oscar De Priest's election in 1928 as a representative from Chicago marked a new era in black political organization in northern cities. De Priest was born in Florence, Alabama, on March 9, 1871. In 1878 the De Priest family, along with thousands of other Mississippi Valley blacks, moved to Kansas. De Priest graduated from elementary school in Salina and enrolled in a business course at the Salina Normal school, where he learned the trade of bookkeeping. About 1889 he settled in Chicago, becoming an apprentice plasterer, house painter and decorator and eventually established his own business and a real estate management firm. By 1904 De Priest's ability to bargain for and deliver the black vote in the Second and Third wards gained him a seat on the Cook County Board of Commissioners.

From 1915 to 1917 De Priest was a member

of the Chicago City Council. He resigned from office after being indicted on charges of accepting protection money, but with Clarence Darrow as a defense counsel, he won acquittal. In 1918 and 1919 he failed to regain his council seat as an independent candidate challenging the regular black Republican candidates. De Priest recovered enough power by 1924 to be elected Third Ward Committeeman. Following the death of First District Representative Martin Madden in April 1928, De Priest was chosen by his fellow Third Ward Committeemen as the Republican nominee for the congressional vacancy. In the November election he defeated Democrat Harry Baker and a third candidate, William Harrison, to become the first black elected to Congress in 30 years and the first ever from outside the South.

The arrival of the new black congressman immediately challenged the strict segregation that pervaded every aspect of Washington life in the early twentieth century. Two southern members insisted that they would not accept offices adjacent to De Priest's. When Mrs. Hoover invited Mrs. De Priest to a White House tea for congressional wives, the appearance of a black woman as a guest in the Executive Mansion provoked a wave of denunciation across the South.

De Priest took his seat in the Seventy-first Congress on April 15, 1929, and served on the Committees on Enrolled Bills, Indian Affairs and Invalid Pensions. He echoed the words of the last black to have served in the House, George Henry White, by proposing that Congress reduce the number of seats held by states that disfranchised black citizens. In March 1931 De Priest introduced a bill providing for a seventy-five dollar monthly pension to ex-slave citizens above the age of seventy-five, to be distributed under the direction of the Veterans' Administration. He also called on Congress to make Abraham Lincoln's birthday a legal public holiday. Like other Republicans, De Priest resisted federal programs for economic relief in the Depression, preferring to focus such efforts on the state and community level. De Priest also tried to make the states and counties responsible for the prevention of lynching. Unsuccessful legislation he introduced in 1934 would have fined and imprisoned local authorities if prisoners held under their jurisdiction were lynched. In March 1933 De Priest succeeded in having an anti-discrimination rider added to a $300 million unemployment relief and reforestation measure. He also introduced a joint resolution authorizing federal courts to change the venue of cases if a defendants' right to a fair trial was prejudiced by considerations of race, color, or creed.

In January 1934 Representative Lindsay C. Warren, a Democrat from North Carolina and chairman of the House Committee on Accounts ordered De Priest's private secretary, Morris W. Lewis, and Lewis' son expelled from the House's "whites only" public restaurant. A separate public facility reserved for blacks was operated in the House basement, next to the kitchen. De Priest introduced a resolution calling for an official investigation. In order to circumvent a hostile Rules Committee, he garnered the required 145 signatures calling on the full House to form an investigatory committee. The five-member panel split along party lines, three Democrats against two Republicans, in refusing to recommend any revisions in the House restaurant policy of segregation.

The presidential campaign of Franklin Roosevelt and dissatisfaction with Republican response to the Depression convinced many black Americans to abandon the party of Lincoln and join the Democratic ranks. In the congressional elections of 1934, De Priest faced a formidable challenge from Arthur W. Mitchell, an ardent supporter of Roosevelt and New Deal relief measures. Mitchell attacked De Priest's refusal to vote for emergency federal aid to the poor and criticized De Priest's ineffective protest of segregation in the House restaurant. Mitchell defeated De Priest, becoming the first black Democrat elected to Congress. Two years later De Priest failed to regain his seat from Mitchell. In 1943 De Priest was again elected Third Ward alderman and served once more on the Chicago City Council. Defeated for reelection in 1947, De Priest remained active in his real estate business until his death in Chicago on May 12, 1951.

For further reading:

Day, David S. "Herbert Hoover and Racial Politics: The De Priest Incident." *Journal of Negro History* 65 (Winter 1980): 6-17.

Mann, Kenneth Eugene. "Oscar Stanton De Priest: Persuasive Agent for the Black Masses." *Negro History Bulletin* 35 (October 1972): 134-137.

Rudwick, Elliott M. "Oscar De Priest and the Jim Crow Restaurant in the U.S. House of Representatives." *Journal of Negro Education* 35 (Winter 1966): 77-82.

CHARLES COLES DIGGS, Jr.

(Moorland-Spingarn Research Center, Howard University)

United States Representative

Democrat of Michigan

Eighty-fourth—Ninety-sixth Congresses

Charles Diggs, the first black representative from Michigan, was born in Detroit on December 2, 1922. He was educated in Detroit's public schools and graduated from Miller High School in 1940. The same year he entered the University of Michigan at Ann Arbor and enrolled at Fisk University in the fall of 1942. Diggs entered the United States Army Air Forces as a private on February 19, 1943. He was commissioned a second lieutenant in 1944 and was discharged on June 1, 1945. He enrolled in the Wayne College of Mortuary Science in Detroit in September 1945 and graduated in June of 1946, subsequently becoming a licensed mortician and board chairman of the House of Diggs, Inc. Diggs graduated from Detroit College of Law in 1951. While still a student he was elected to the state senate and served from 1951 to 1954. He defeated incumbent Representative

George D. O'Brien in the August 1954 Democratic primary in Michigan's Thirteenth District and was elected to Congress in November over Landon Knight, the Republican nominee.

Diggs began his congressional career on January 3, 1955, as a member of the Committee on Interior and Insular Affairs and the Veterans' Affairs Committee. He proposed an amendment to the 1938 Fair Labor Standards Act to increase the minimum wage and submitted legislation to alleviate unemployment in economically depressed areas and to establish a federal agency for the handicapped and a youth conservation corps similar to the Civilian Conservation Corps of the 1930s. Diggs attended the September 1955 trial of two white Mississippians accused of murdering fourteen-year old Emmett Till and in November asked President Eisenhower to call a special session of Congress to consider civil rights issues. He called for enforcement of Section Two of the Fourteenth Amendment as a sanction against states that disfranchised black citizens. He supported the Civil Rights Act of 1957. After visiting the two newly integrated high schools of Little Rock, Arkansas, in December 1959, he called on Eisenhower to visit the city on a goodwill tour to ease racial tensions. Along with four other representatives, Diggs joined 12,000 people in Charleston in a May 1969 march supporting black hospital workers who were seeking the right to organize and bargain collectively. The same year he became the founder and chairman of the initial Congressional Black Caucus.

In 1959 Diggs, who continually stressed the importance of black Africa's emerging nations, joined the Committee on Foreign Affairs and a decade later became chairman of its Subcommittee on Africa. He accompanied Vice President Nixon on his 1957 tour of Africa and attended the 1958 All-African Peoples Conference in Accra, Ghana. In February 1969 he headed a fact-finding mission to Nigeria, then in the midst of civil war, to investigate relief programs for civilians and to explore a possible cease-fire. He also held hearings in April to study the Civil Aeronautics Board's decision to provide South African Airways with landing rights in the United States. Named to the United States delegation to the United Nations, Diggs resigned in December 1971 to protest American sales of arms and transport planes to Portuguese and South African forces and the Defense Department's purchase of Rhodesian chrome. In 1973 he became chairman of an eighteen-group coalition lobbying the government to provide $30 million in famine relief to the drought-stricken Sahel region. Diggs' activities led the South African government to refuse him entry into the country during a trip to Africa in 1975.

In 1963 Diggs joined the Committee on the District of Columbia and became its chairman after the 1972 primary defeat of John L. McMillan, a South Carolina segregationist who first chaired the committee in 1945 and blocked all proposals for home rule in Washington, D.C. As chairman Diggs played a major role in securing passage of a measure for partial self-government in the District. On December 24, 1973, President Nixon signed the District of Columbia Self-Government and Governmental Reorganization Act, enabling residents of the nation's capital to elect their mayor and city council for the first time since 1874.

In October 1978 Diggs was convicted in a Washington, D.C., district court on charges of mail fraud and falsifying payroll forms. Following recommendations contained in a report by the Committee on Standards of Official Conduct, the House censured Diggs on July 31, 1979. After the Supreme Court refused to review his conviction, Diggs resigned from the Ninety-sixth Congress on June 3, 1980. He is a resident of Hillcrest Heights, Maryland.

JULIAN C. DIXON

(Office of Representative Dixon)

United States Representative
Democrat of California
Ninety-sixth—One Hundred First Congresses

During his six terms in Congress, Julian C. Dixon has emerged as a leader in a variety of House affairs. Since 1985 he has served as chairman of the Committee on Standards of Official Conduct, also known as the Ethics Committee. On the Appropriations Committee he has served as chairman of the Subcommittee on the District of Columbia since 1980. In the Ninety-eighth Congress he was chairman of the Congressional Black Caucus.

Julian Carey Dixon was born in Washington, D.C., on August 8, 1934. He graduated from public high school in Los Angeles and went on to earn a B.S. at California State University at Los Angeles in 1962 and a law degree from Southwestern University's School of Law in 1967. Dixon's career in politics began not as an elected official but as a legislative aide to California State Senator Mervyn Dymally, now a fellow House Member. In

1972 Dixon won election to the California state assembly and served there until he entered the House of Representatives in 1979. In the state house, he was chairman of the assembly Democratic caucus.

In addition to serving as chairman of the Appropriations Subcommittee on the District of Columbia, Dixon sits on the Subcommittees on Defense and on Military Construction. Prior to the 100th Congress, Dixon served on the Appropriations Subcommittee on Foreign Operations, a position that enabled him to influence United States assistance abroad. During his tenure on this subcommittee, he wrote the first economic sanctions law against South Africa. He also has been instrumental in gaining increased development assistance for Africa, disaster assistance for Jamaica, and scholarships for disadvantaged South African students. Throughout his term in the House, Dixon has taken a particular interest in legislation related to mass transit, low and moderate income housing, and health care.

In addition to his leadership positions in Congress, Dixon served as chairman of the Rules Committee of the Democratic National Convention in 1984. He currently serves as president of the Congressional Black Caucus Foundation, Inc.

MERVYN MALCOLM DYMALLY

(Office of Representative Dymally)

United States Representative
Democrat of California
Ninety-seventh—One Hundred First Congresses

Mervyn M. Dymally became a Member of the House of Representatives in 1981 following a diverse career in education and government. He was born in Cedros, Trinidad, in the British West Indies, on May 12, 1926. He attended Cedros Government School on Trinidad and St. Benedict and Naparima secondary schools in San Fernando, Trinidad. In 1946 he arrived in the United States to study at Lincoln University in Jefferson City, Missouri.

He earned a B.A. degree in education from California State University, Los Angeles, in 1954. In 1956 he began a career as a teacher of exceptional children in Los Angeles.

From 1963 to 1966 Dymally served in the California assembly, and was a member of the state senate from 1967 until 1975. As a state senator, he chaired committees on social welfare, military and veterans affairs, elections and reapportionment, and a select committee on medical education and health needs. While a member of the legislature, he earned a M.A. degree in government at California State University at Sacramento in 1969. In 1974 he was elected lieutenant governor of California and headed the State Commission for Economic Development and the Commission of the Californias. He was an unsuccessful candidate for reelection in 1978. In 1978 he received a Ph.D. degree in human behavior from United States International University in San Diego.

Dymally defeated Representative Charles H. Wilson and three other candidates in the June 1980 primary in California's Thirty-first Congressional District and was decisively elected in November. He presently serves on the House Foreign Affairs Committee, chairing its Subcommittee on International Operations. He also serves on the Post Office and Civil Service Committee and the District of Columbia Committee, chairing its Subcommittee on Judiciary and Education. From 1987 until 1989 he was chairman of the Congressional Black Caucus. Dymally has sponsored legislation advocating the causes of many human rights groups and has devoted particular attention to United States policies toward and assistance levels to nations in Africa and the Caribbean. He has also called for increased funding for the education of minority students and senior citizens and for expanded opportunities for minority-owned and operated energy firms to develop oil and gas resources on federal land.

ROBERT BROWN ELLIOTT

(Library of Congress)

United States Representative
Republican of South Carolina
Forty-second—Forty-third Congresses

Robert Brown Elliott of South Carolina was one of the most talented and controversial politicians of his generation. During his prominent career in Reconstruction politics, Elliott offered conflicting accounts of his early life. His claim of birth in Boston and service in the Union Army allowed him to enter politics soon after arriving in South Carolina, but no evidence confirms his story. Elliott was probably born in 1842 in Liverpool, England, received an education there, and learned the typesetter's trade. He served in the British navy and arrived in Boston about 1867. The same year he moved to Charleston and went to work for future Congressman Richard H. Cain as associate editor of the *South Carolina Leader*. Elliott was a leading figure at the 1868 state constitutional convention, where he advocated compulsory public education and defeated the imposition of a poll tax and literacy test for voters.

In 1868 Elliott was elected to the state house of representatives. While serving in that body he studied law and was admitted to the South Carolina bar in September. On March 25, 1869, Governor Robert K. Scott appointed Elliott assistant adjutant general of South Carolina, with authority to organize a state militia to protect citizens from Ku Klux Klan violence. Over the next year, however, Elliott came to believe that Scott was using the militia to advance his own political career, and he resigned in December 1870.

In July 1870 Third District Republicans nominated Elliott for Congress over the incumbent representative, Solomon L. Hoge. Elliott defeated John E. Bacon, candidate of the Democrats, who were then calling themselves the "Union Reform" party.

Upon entering the Forty-second Congress in March 1871 Elliott took a seat on the Committee on Education and Labor. In his first House speech on March 14 he challenged an amnesty bill then before Congress. Elliott urged the House to delay the restoration of political rights for ex-Confederates and concentrate on protecting loyal citizens in southern states. Outraged by Ku Klux Klan activities in South Carolina, and particularly by the Klan's murder of six blacks jailed for the killing of a white whiskey peddler, Elliott delivered an impassioned speech in favor of an act of 1871 restricting the Klan's influence.

In 1872 Elliott was reelected without opposition, gaining almost ninety-three percent of the vote. In November he tried to become the first black to win a full term in the United States Senate, but was defeated in the state general assembly after his opponent, John J. Patterson, spent money freely to win over legislators.

In the Forty-third Congress Elliott continued to sit on the Education and Labor Committee and was also named to the Committee on the Militia. On January 5, 1874, Elliott gained national attention for a speech in support of the omnibus civil rights bill. Replying to Georgia Representative (and former Confederate vice president) Alexander Stephens,

he interpreted the recent Slaughter-House Cases of the Supreme Court as a reaffirmation of the right and duty of Congress to legislate against discrimination. He concluded by evoking the sacrifices of the Civil War and asserting that the war's true meaning lay in the struggle to secure liberty and equal rights for any American citizen who had experienced discrimination.

When he returned to South Carolina in February Elliott was acclaimed by blacks as a hero, but he realized that corruption and internal divisions within the state Republican party were bolstering Democratic fortunes and endangering the prospects for black participation in politics. To lead effectively the drive for reform Elliott needed to remain in South Carolina, and on November 1, 1874, he resigned his House seat and won a seat in the state general assembly.

As speaker of the assembly, Elliott tried but failed to stem the tide of violence, intimidation and economic pressure undermining blacks' civil rights and their representation in state government. To make matters worse, the Republican governor, Daniel Chamberlain, was increasingly identified with the state's Democrats in spite of the fact that he had been elected with heavy support from black voters. In 1876 Elliott was elected state attorney general, but the withdrawal of federal troops and collapse of the Chamberlain administration the following April made Elliott's position increasingly untenable. With the end of federal Reconstruction, Elliott was forced out of office in May 1877.

Elliott returned to his law practice, but found business for black attorneys to be so meager that in 1879 he accepted an appointment as a special customs inspector for the Treasury Department, based in Charleston. While on an inspection trip to Florida he suffered the first of the malarial fever attacks which gradually undermined his health. He worked for Secretary of the Treasury John Sherman's presidential campaign, seconding his nomination and serving as manager of Sherman's black delegates at the Republican Convention of 1880. In May 1881 the Treasury Department transferred Elliott to New Orleans. His disenchantment with the move from South Carolina intensified and led to his dismissal in August 1882. He established another law partnership, but it failed to prosper. Elliott, with none of the public influence he enjoyed as a politician, lapsed into poverty before his death in New Orleans on August 9, 1884.

For further reading:

Lamson, Peggy. *The Glorious Failure: Black Congressman Robert Brown Elliott and the Reconstruction in South Carolina.* New York: W.W. Norton and Co., Inc., 1973.

Miller, M. Sammye. "Elliott of South Carolina: Lawyer and Legislator." *Negro History Bulletin* 36 (May 1973): pp. 112–114.

MIKE ESPY

(Office of Representative Espy)

United States Representative
Democrat of Mississippi
One Hundredth—One Hundred First Congresses

In 1987, Mike Espy, a native of the Mississippi Delta with strong family ties to the region, was sworn in as the state's first black congressman since John R. Lynch served over one hundred years before. Although a black candidate had failed to win the seat in two previous attempts, Espy defeated the incumbent in the state's only black majority district in his first campaign. He easily won reelection to the One Hundred First Congress.

Albert Michael Espy was born in Yazoo City, Mississippi, on November 30, 1953. As an undergraduate he attended Howard University where he received a B.A. degree in 1975. He graduated with a J.D. from the University of Santa Clara School of Law in 1978. Espy returned to practice in his native state and served as assistant secretary of state for Mississippi Legal Services from 1978 to 1980. He was assistant secretary of state of the Public

Lands Division from 1980 to 1984 and assistant state attorney general of the Consumer Protection Division in 1984 and 1985.

Espy's administrative experience in Mississippi government and organizational support throughout the Delta laid the foundation for his successful run for a House seat. In the One Hundredth Congress, Espy gained committee assignments that were particularly favorable for his district which is predominantly rural and has one of the nation's highest rates of poverty. Espy serves on the Agriculture Committee, the Budget Committee, and the Select Committee on Hunger. In his freshman term he sponsored the Lower Mississippi River Valley Delta Development Act.

MELVIN HERBERT EVANS

(Congressional Black Caucus)

Delegate
Republican of the Virgin Islands
Ninety-sixth Congress

Melvin Evans achieved distinction as the first popularly elected governor of the Virgin Islands and as a physician and public health official before his election to Congress. He was born in Christiansted, St. Croix, on August 7, 1917, soon after the United States had purchased the Islands from Denmark. After graduating from high school on St. Thomas, Evans received a B.S in 1940 from Howard University and an M.D. from the Howard College of Medicine in 1944. During the next fifteen years he served in a variety of medical and public health posts at hospitals and institutions in the United States and the Virgin Islands. From 1959 to 1967 Evans served as the Islands' health commissioner. He returned to private practice for two years before President Nixon appointed him governor of the Islands. In August 1968 Congress passed the Virgin Islands Elective Governor Act, providing for the election of a governor by the territory's residents. Evans was elected as a Republican to the governor's office in 1970 and served until 1975. After his unsuccessful bid for reelection in 1974 he was Republican National Committeeman from the Virgin Islands and chairman of the board of trustees of the College of the Virgin Islands.

In 1978 Evans was elected to the House over Janet Watlington. He was sworn into the Ninety-sixth Congress on January 3, 1979, and served on the Armed Services, Interior and Insular Affairs, and Merchant Marine and Fisheries Committees. During his congressional career he paid close attention to the needs of his unique constituency. He secured federal funds to provide the Virgin Islands' public education system with additional programs and services for its expanding school-age population. Evans introduced legislation to alleviate the Islands' critical shortage of doctors at local health facilities by permitting foreign physicians to practice there. He attempted to make farm credit loans available to local fishing and agricultural industries and succeeded in having the Islands included under the definition of a "state" so that they would receive full law enforcement funding. Following the devastation wrought by Hurricane David and Tropical Storm Frederick, he urged Congress to approve flood control measures for the Islands.

Evans spoke to the House on national issues as well, favoring efforts to designate a legal national holiday honoring Martin Luther King, Jr. After the death of A. Philip Randolph in May 1979, he was among those who eulogized the civil rights leader. He opposed a constitutional amendment eliminating court-ordered busing in public schools, criticizing proponents of the amendment for not offering a workable alternative to busing and stating that the practice ought to continue until such an alternative was found.

Evans was defeated in his 1980 reelection bid by Ron de Lugo. In 1981 he was appointed United States Ambassador to Trinidad and Tobago and served in that office until his death in Christiansted on November 27, 1984.

WALTER EDWARD FAUNTROY

(Office of Representative Fauntroy)

Delegate
Democrat of the District of Columbia
Ninety-second—One Hundred First Congresses

On April 19, 1971, Walter Fauntroy became the District of Columbia's first elected representative in the United States Congress since the brief service of Norton P. Chipman a century earlier. Born in Washington on February 6, 1933, Fauntroy graduated from Dunbar High School in 1952 and earned a B.A. degree at Virginia Union University in 1955. After receiving a Bachelor of Divinity degree from Yale University Divinity School in 1958, he became the minister of Washington's New Bethel Baptist Church, where he continues to serve.

In 1960 Fauntroy was appointed by Dr. Martin Luther King, Jr., as director of the Washington Bureau of the Southern Christian Leadership Conference, and was the District of Columbia coordinator of the historic August 28, 1963, March on Washington for Jobs and Freedom. He served as coordinator of the 1965 march from Selma to Montgomery, Alabama, and as national coordinator of the 1968 Poor People's Campaign. Fauntroy also centered many of his civil rights, antipoverty and neighborhood revitalization activities on the nation's capital as the founder and director of the Shaw Urban Renewal Project.

Fauntroy's first political office was that of vice chair of the District of Columbia Council, in which he served from 1967 until his resignation in 1969 to spend more time with the Model Inner City Community Organization, a neighborhood planning agency he had founded with other Washington ministers. The following year Congress passed the District of Columbia Delegate Act, which again provided for Washington's representation in the House of Representatives. Fauntroy won the Democratic nomination for this post in January 1971 and was overwhelmingly elected in March. After entering the House he began work on comprehensive legislation for home rule for Washington. The District of Columbia Self-Government and Governmental Reorganization Act became law in December 1973 and gave the District limited self rule, permitting citizens to elect a mayor and city council. Fauntroy has continued to pursue full representation for the District's citizens in both houses of Congress.

Fauntroy currently chairs the District of Columbia Committee's Subcommittee on Fiscal Affairs and Health. He also belongs to the Committee on Banking, Finance and Urban Affairs and is chairman of its Subcommittee on International Development Institutions and Finance. In this capacity he has supported legislation to make affordable housing more widely available. During the 97th Congress (1981–1983) he was elected chairman of the Congressional Black Caucus. He has cosponsored anti-drug bills as a member of the House Select Committee on Narcotics and has also been involved in efforts to end minority rule in South Africa and to restore human rights and promote economic development in Haiti.

FLOYD HAROLD FLAKE

(Office of Representative Flake)

United States Representative
Democrat of New York
One Hundredth—One Hundred First Congresses

Floyd Flake's seat in the One Hundredth Congress was his first political office and the latest step in a diverse career marked by community involvement. As pastor of the Allen A.M.E. Church in Jamaica, N.Y., from 1976 to 1986, Flake helped direct a variety of local projects including construction of a senior citizens' complex, creation of a housing rehabilitation corporation, and establishment of a home health care service. During his tenure, church membership increased from 1,400 to more than 5,000.

Flake was born in Los Angeles on January 30, 1945, and attended public schools in Houston, Texas. After graduating from Wilberforce University in 1967, Flake undertook graduate work at Payne Theological Seminary in Ohio and studied business administration at Northeastern University in Boston. In the years between academic study, he worked as a salesman, a marketing analyst, assistant dean of students at Lincoln University, and director of the Afro-American Center and university chaplain at Boston University.

After a decade of community leadership as a minister, Flake entered the race for the congressional seat left vacant by the death of Representative Joseph Addabbo. He narrowly lost the Democratic primary to Alton Waldon who won the special election in June of 1986 and took his seat in the closing months of the Ninety-ninth Congress. Flake returned to defeat Waldon in the primary for the Democratic nomination to the One Hundredth Congress. Flake easily defeated his Republican opponent in November 1986 and won reelection to the One Hundred First Congress.

In his first congressional term, Flake enjoyed committee assignments that coincided with his community interests in New York. He serves on the Banking, Finance and Urban Affairs Committee, the Committee on Small Business, and the Select Committee on Hunger.

HAROLD EUGENE FORD

(Office of Representative Ford)

United States Representative
Democrat of Tennessee
Ninety-fourth—One Hundred First Congresses

Soon after Harold Ford entered his family's mortuary business he followed the other family tradition of involvement in Tennessee politics. At the age of twenty-five he won election to the state house of representatives and served as majority whip during his first term. In 1974 the twenty-nine year old Ford narrowly defeated a Republican incumbent to become Tennessee's first black Member of the U.S. House of Representatives. In subsequent elections, Ford expanded his support and gained a secure seat in the Ninth District.

The eighth of fifteen children, Harold Eugene Ford was born on May 20, 1945, in Memphis to a prominent local family. In preparation for work in the family business, he earned a B.S. in business administration from Tennessee State University in 1967 and an A.A. in mortuary science from John Gupton College in 1969. Since entering Congress he returned to school and graduated with an M.B.A. from Howard University in 1982.

Originally appointed a member of the Committee on Banking, Currency and Housing and the Veterans' Affairs Committee, in his second term Ford left those committees for a seat on the powerful Ways and Means Committee. He took a special interest in the committee's jurisdiction over welfare legislation. In 1981 he was elected to chair the Ways and Means Subcommittee on Public Assistance and Unemployment Compensation. The subcommittee has jurisdiction over such programs as Aid to Families with Dependent Children, Child Welfare and Foster Care, Low Income Energy Assistance and Unemployment Compensation Insurance. From this chair, Ford has been able to introduce a comprehensive welfare reform bill. He also serves on the Select Committee on Aging. Speaker of the House Jim Wright appointed Ford a member of the Democratic Steering and Policy Committee in 1987.

WILLIAM HERBERT GRAY III

(Office of Representative Gray)

United States Representative
Democrat of Pennsylvania
Ninety-sixth—One Hundred First Congresses

The first black congressman to hold one of the principal positions in the Democratic leadership, William Gray was born in Baton Rouge, Louisiana, on August 20, 1941, and was raised in Florida and north Philadelphia. Following graduation from Simon Gratz High School in 1959 Gray received a B.A. degree from Franklin and Marshall College in 1963, a Masters in Divinity from Drew Theological Seminary in 1966 and a Masters in Theology from Princeton Theological Seminary in 1970.

In 1964 Gray became minister of Union Baptist Church in Montclair, New Jersey, serving until 1972 when he assumed the pastorate of Philadelphia's Bright Hope Baptist Church. He also taught at St. Peter's College, Jersey City State College, Rutgers University and Montclair State College. While serving in Montclair and Philadelphia Gray founded non-profit corporations to build affordable housing for low and moderate-income tenants.

Gray made his first bid for public office in 1976, when he narrowly lost the nomination in the Second Congressional District to ten-term Representative Robert N.C. Nix, Sr. Gray defeated Nix in the May 1978 primary and won the November election by a wide margin. He became a member of the Ninety-sixth Congress on January 3, 1979, and served on the Budget Committee, the Committee on the District of Columbia and the Committee on Foreign Affairs. During his second term in 1981 he joined the Committee on Appropriations and became a member of the Democratic Steering and Policy Committee.

While on the foreign affairs panel Gray secured legislation for the creation of the African Development Foundation for direct delivery of American aid to villages on the continent. In 1983 he sponsored a series of set-aside provisions guaranteeing minority and women-owned businesses, minority private agencies and historically black colleges greater participation in programs administered by the Agency for International Development. Gray's interest in African affairs helped make him one of the first public officials to warn of impending famine in Ethiopia. In 1984 the House approved a bill he sponsored providing for emergency food aid to that nation.

In January 1985 Gray was elected chairman of the House Budget Committee and served in that position throughout the Ninety-ninth and One Hundredth Congresses, guiding four successive Democratic budget resolutions through the House. In 1981 and 1982 he was vice chair of the Congressional Black Caucus. Gray was the chief sponsor of the Anti-Apartheid Act passed by the House in June 1985, which called for a ban on United States bank loans and computer exports to South Africa.

At the close of the One Hundredth Congress, as Gray ended his appointed term as chairman of the Budget Committee, he was elected chairman of the House Democratic Caucus. Six months later, in June 1989, he was elected Democratic Whip.

KATIE BEATRICE HALL

(Congressional Black Caucus)

*United States Representative
Democrat of Indiana
Ninety-seventh—Ninety-eighth Congresses*

Katie Hall was the first black representative from Indiana. She was born Katie Beatrice Greene on April 3, 1938, in Mound Bayou, Mississippi. After attending public schools in Mound Bayou she received a B.S. from Mississippi Valley State University in 1960 and an M.S. from Indiana University in 1968. She taught in the public schools of Gary, Indiana, from 1961 to 1975. She also worked in the mayoral campaigns of Richard Hatcher of 1967, 1971 and 1975, and served as chair of the Lake County Democratic Committee from 1978 to 1980. She served in the Indiana House of Representatives from 1974 to 1976 and in the Indiana Senate from 1976 to 1982.

Following the death of Representative Adam Benjamin, Jr., in September 1982, Hatcher, the Democratic chairman of the First Congressional District Democratic committee, was designated by Indiana law to select a candidate to run for both the remainder of Benjamin's term in the Ninety-seventh Congress and for a full term in the Ninety-eighth Congress. When he chose Hall, the chairmen of three counties in the district filed a suit to have her candidacy decertified, charging that they had not been consulted during the selection process. A circuit court judge, however, ruled that Hall was entitled to the nomination. She defeated the Republican candidate, Thomas H. Krieger, in the November 2, 1982, election, thereby becoming a member of the Ninety-seventh and Ninety-eighth Congresses. She served on the Committee on the Post Office and Civil Service and the Committee on Public Works and Transportation.

For much of her congressional tenure, Hall was concerned with the effects that economic recession and the market penetration of imported steel were having on the welfare of her constituents. Speaking to the House in June 1983, she observed that widespread layoffs and plant closings drove the unemployment rate in the First District to twenty-five percent. Calling unemployment the most serious problem facing America, Hall pointed to its side effects—mortgage foreclosures, divorce, mental illness and child and spouse abuse—and asked for passage of legislation to protect the steel industry from imports and encourage exports of domestically produced steel. She also spoke in favor of the proposed Equal Rights Amendment to the Constitution and called on South Africa to abandon its policy of removing blacks from their ancestral homelands to so-called "black spots" in barren areas far from the cities. On July 29, 1983, Hall introduced an act to make the birthday of Martin Luther King, Jr., a legal public holiday. The bill passed the House in August and the Senate in October before being signed into law by President Reagan the following month.

In the Democratic primary of 1984 Hall lost to Peter J. Visclosky in her bid for renomination. She remained active in civic and political affairs, serving as vice chair of the Gary Housing Board Commissioners and as a state senator from the Third District of Indiana.

JEREMIAH HARALSON

(Library of Congress)

United States Representative
Republican of Alabama
Forty-fourth Congress

Jeremiah Haralson was born a slave near Columbus, Georgia, on April 1, 1846. In 1859 he was taken to Alabama as a slave of John Haralson and remained in bondage until 1865. After attaining freedom he taught himself to read and write. Limited written records suggest Haralson became a farmer and may also have been a clergyman. What is clear is that the young man emerged as a powerful, confident orator and adroit debater. At the age of twenty-two, Haralson made his first bid for Congress in 1868 but was unsuccessful. In 1870 he ran as an independent for the state house of representatives and defeated a Republican candidate for the seat. Haralson was the presiding officer of the First Congressional District convention that nominated Benjamin S. Turner for his successful campaign to become Alabama's first black representative. In 1870 the Twenty-first District elected Haralson to the state senate, and two years later he urged black voters to spurn the Liberal Republican movement and remain loyal to the reelection campaign of President Grant. In 1874 Haralson was elected to Congress over Liberal Republican Frederick G. Bromberg, who had unseated Turner two years earlier. Bromberg charged that Haralson received fraudulent votes while his own supporters were intimidated at the polls or prevented from voting. The House Committee on Elections ruled unanimously in April 1876 that while some votes for Haralson were invalid, he still held enough to win the election. The Democratic-controlled House sustained the committee's decision.

Haralson took his seat in the Forty-fourth Congress on March 4, 1875, and served on the Committee on Public Expenditures. He delivered no speeches on the House floor but introduced several pieces of legislation, including a bill to use proceeds from public land sales for educational purposes and a bill for the relief of the Medical College of Alabama. He also presented a petition from citizens in Mobile requesting compensation for use of a medical college building and supplies by officers of the Freedmen's Bureau. When the lame-duck session of the Forty-fourth Congress began in January 1877, Haralson presented petitions from citizens of Clarke County, Alabama, for the establishment of a post route from Bay-Minette to Suggsville.

Haralson differed from many in his own party when he criticized the use of federal soldiers to control violence and ensure orderly voting in the South during the 1876 election. He also was in favor of a general amnesty for former Confederates. In the crucial year of 1876 he stood for reelection from a new congressional district, the Fourth, which had been gerrymandered so that it was the only Alabama district with a black majority. In a three-way contest that included Haralson on an independent ticket and former Representative James T. Rapier as a Republican, the Democrat, Charles M. Shelley, won the seat. Haralson contested the results before the House, but the Committee on Elections ruled in Shelley's favor. Haralson unsuccessfully challenged Shelley again in 1878.

After leaving Congress Haralson was a clerk at Baltimore's federal custom house and a clerk in the Department of the Interior. He worked for the Pension Bureau in Washington from 1882 to 1884 before moving to Louisiana and taking up farming. In 1904 he went to Arkansas where he worked briefly as a pension agent. By 1912 he returned to Alabama and settled in Selma, but soon thereafter began his years as a wanderer, drifting to Texas, then to Oklahoma and Colorado, where he took up coal mining. Haralson was apparently killed by wild animals near Denver about 1916, but no official records confirm his death.

AUGUSTUS FREEMAN HAWKINS

(Office of Representative Hawkins)

*United States Representative
Democrat of California
Eighty-eighth—One Hundred First Congresses*

With his reelection to the One Hundred First Congress, Augustus "Gus" Hawkins ranks with William Dawson as the longest serving black members of Congress. Hawkins' longevity in office and his legislative accomplishments have gained him widespread influence in the House of Representatives. He became chairman of the Committee on House Administration in the Ninety-seventh Congress and concurrently served as chairman of the Joint Committee on the Library in the Ninety-seventh Congress and the Joint Committee on Printing in the Ninety-eighth Congress. In the Ninety-eighth Congress Hawkins assumed the chairmanship of the Committee on Education and Labor and thus achieved new authority over the legislative issues that have always been his greatest interest.

Hawkins embarked on his lengthy career in the House after twenty-eight years as a member of the California assembly. He had lived in California since his family moved there from Louisiana when he was eleven. Hawkins' father was born in England and established himself as a pharmacist in Shreveport following several African expeditions. Gus Hawkins was born in Shreveport on August 31, 1907. He graduated from high school in Los Angeles and received his undergraduate degree from the University of California at Los Angeles in 1931.

In the California assembly from 1935 to 1963 Hawkins compiled the kind of substantive legislative record that also marks his career in the House of Representatives. In addition to serving as chair of the assembly's rules committee, he introduced a fair housing act, a fair employment practices act, low-cost housing and disability insurance legislation, and workmen's compensation provisions for domestic workers.

Hawkins' election to Congress in 1962 made him the first black representative from any western state. From his seat on the Committee on Education and Labor he continued to sponsor legislation designed to create jobs and insure civil rights. Among the most notable accomplishments of his early years in the House was the establishment of the Equal Employment Opportunity Commission in Title VII of the Civil Rights Act of 1964. He is perhaps best known for authoring the Full Employment and Balanced Growth Act of 1978, also known as the Humphrey-Hawkins Act. In addition to authorizing numerous labor and education bills in more than a quarter century in Congress, Hawkins succeeded in restoring an honorable discharge for the 167 black soldiers dismissed from the Twenty-fifth Infantry Regiment of the U.S. Army after being falsely accused of public disturbance in Brownsville, Texas, in 1906.

CHARLES ARTHUR HAYES

(Office of Representative Hayes)

United States Representative
Democrat of Illinois
Ninety-eighth—One Hundred First Congresses

After more than forty-five years as a trade unionist, Charles Hayes succeeded Harold Washington in the House when Washington was elected mayor of Chicago. Born in Cairo, Illinois, on February 17, 1918, Hayes graduated from Cairo's Sumner High School in 1935. While working in Cairo as a machine operator, he helped organize Local 1424 of the United Brotherhood of Carpenters and Joiners of America and served as its president from 1940 to 1942. In 1943 Hayes joined the grievance committee of the United Packinghouse Workers of America (U.P.W.A.) and became a U.P.W.A. field representative in 1949. Hayes served as district director for the U.P.W.A.'s District One from 1954 to 1968, when he became a district director and an international vice president of the newly merged packinghouse and meat cutters' unions. From 1979 until his retirement in

September 1983, Hayes was the International Vice President and Director of Region Twelve of the United Food and Commercial Workers International Union. In addition to seeking increased benefits and improved conditions for workers, Hayes also fought to eliminate segregation and discrimination in hiring and promotion in industry. Hayes also sought to provide black and women workers with opportunities to serve as leaders in the labor movement.

Following Washington's resignation from the House in April 1983, Hayes defeated fourteen opponents in a special primary and was elected in August to represent the First Congressional District, which covers much of south central Chicago. He was sworn in as a member of the Ninety-eighth Congress on September 12, 1983, and currently serves on the Committee on Education and Labor and the Small Business Committee. During his congressional career Hayes has introduced several pieces of legislation to address the educational and employment needs of many Americans. Prominent among these are acts to encourage school drop-outs to reenter and complete their education and to provide disadvantaged young people with job training and support services. Hayes also has sponsored bills to reduce high unemployment rates and make it easier for municipalities to offer affordable utility rates through the purchase of local utility companies. He consistently has opposed the actions and programs of South Africa's white-minority government and in 1984 joined other demonstrators at its Washington embassy in protest of the Pretoria regime's policies of racial separation.

JOHN ADAMS HYMAN

(Moorland-Spingarn Research Center, Howard University)

United States Representative
Republican of North Carolina
Forty-fourth Congress

John Adams Hyman was the first black representative from North Carolina. He was born a slave near Warrenton, North Carolina, on July 23, 1840. In his early twenties, Hyman worked for a Warrenton jeweler named King, who taught him to read and write. When this became known to some whites, they forced King and his wife to leave the community, and Hyman was sold to an Alabama slaveholder. While a slave, Hyman was said to have been sold over eight times because he continued to incur his owners' wrath by pursuing an education. After emancipation, Hyman returned to Warrenton in March 1865, took up farming, and became active in the movement to secure political rights for North Carolina blacks.

Although he was only twenty-six, Hyman served on two committees at the Freedmen's Convention of North Carolina in 1865 and was a delegate to the March 1867 Republican State Convention. While the convention was in session Hyman was named to the Republican party state executive committee. In November 1867 Hyman was elected a delegate from Warren County to the North Carolina Constitutional Convention which met at Raleigh the following January. He was one of the fifteen black delegates in the 133-member body and was appointed to the internal improvements committee. The same year he was elected to the state senate and helped persuade Warren County blacks to ignore threats and vote for the new state constitution. In a legislature already divided by factions, Hyman faced unsubstantiated charges from Conservatives and Democrats who claimed he had accepted bribes from railroad lobbyists.

By 1872 Hyman ran for the Republican nomination for the House from the predominantly black Second Congressional District. He was defeated by Charles R. Thomas, but in 1874 he captured the nomination from Thomas and easily won election over Democrat George W. Blount. After Blount challenged the election's outcome, Hyman was forced to spend much of his congressional term absent from the House in order to prepare a defense. On August 1, 1876, the House unanimously rejected Blount's claim to Hyman's seat.

While in the House Hyman served on the Committee on Manufactures. He sponsored legislation authorizing the Treasury Department to build a lighthouse at Gull Rock on Pamlico Sound in North Carolina and introduced measures to compensate constituents for losses incurred during the Civil War. He also sought financial relief for Cherokee Indians who had resettled in the west. All of Hyman's legislative initiatives failed to pass beyond the committee stage.

Hyman lost his bid for renomination to former governor Curtis Brogden at the district convention in July 1876. He soon resumed farming and ran a grocery and liquor store. When not involved in business, Hyman devoted much of his time to the Colored Masons of North Carolina. He also served as a steward and Sunday school superintendent for the Warrenton Colored Methodist Church, but when he was expelled on charges of selling alcoholic beverages and embezzling Sunday school funds, he left Warrenton. Hyman worked as a mail clerks' assistant in Maryland for a decade and moved in 1889 to Washington, where he went to work in the Department of Agriculture's seed dispensary. He died at his home in Washington, D.C., on September 14, 1891.

For further reading:

Reid, George W. "Four in Black: North Carolina's Black Congressmen, 1874–1901." *Journal of Negro History* 64 (Summer 1979): pp. 229–243.

BARBARA CHARLINE JORDAN

(U.S. House of Representatives)

United States Representative
Democrat of Texas
Ninety-third—Ninety-fifth Congress

Barbara Jordan, the first black representative from Texas, was born in Houston on February 21, 1936. She was educated in the public schools of Houston and graduated from Phillis Wheatley High School in 1952. After receiving a B.A. in political science and history from Texas Southern University in 1956 and an LL.B. from Boston University School of Law in 1959, she was admitted to the Massachusetts and Texas bars and commenced practice in Houston in 1960. She was an unsuccessful candidate for nomination as state representative in 1962 and 1964. During 1964 and 1965 she served as administrative assistant to Harris County Judge Bill Elliott and as project coordinator of a non-profit corporation to help the unemployed. In 1966 she became the first black person since 1883 to serve in the Texas Senate and was reelected in 1968.

In 1972 Jordan defeated Republican Paul

Merritt to represent Texas' Eighteenth District in the House of Representatives. She was a member of the Judiciary committee in the Ninety-third Congress and also joined the Committee on Government Operations during the Ninety-fourth and Ninety-fifth Congresses.

Shortly after the Ninety-third Congress convened in 1973, it entered a struggle with the Nixon administration over budgetary reform, the troubled economy, Indochina and other issues. Jordan and other freshman representatives met with Speaker Carl Albert and arranged a meeting on the House floor in April to provide newly elected Democrats an opportunity to express their frustration with the difficult relations between Congress and the executive. Jordan herself praised the House's capacity for self-reform and called on it to make the difficult choices necessary to govern effectively. During the same Congress she attached civil rights amendments to legislation authorizing cities to receive direct Law Enforcement Assistance Administration grants, rather than apply to state governments for the money. Jordan questioned the civil rights record of House Republican leader Gerald Ford when he was nominated for vice president, and joined seven other Judiciary Committee members in voting against his confirmation. During the Judiciary Committee's hearings on the possible impeachment of President Nixon in the summer of 1974, Jordan won national acclaim for her eloquent reaffirmation of faith in the Constitution while voting for all five articles of impeachment.

In June 1975 the House voted to extend the Voting Rights Act of 1965 for ten years. Jordan sponsored legislation extending the Act to include Spanish-heritage, American Indian, Alaskan Natives and Asian American language minorities, while opposing amendments that would have permitted states and localities covered or partially covered by the Act to apply for exemption. She secured passage of the Consumer Goods Pricing Act of 1975, her bill repealing anti-trust exemptions that allowed states to enact "fair trade" laws that kept consumer prices artificially high. Jordan also favored a $25 billion extension of the general federal revenue sharing program and worked to toughen its anti-discrimination provisions. In July 1976 she became the first black and the first woman to deliver a keynote address to the Democratic National Convention. The following year she co-sponsored legislation to extend the state ratification deadline for the proposed Equal Rights Amendment from 1979 to 1986.

In December 1977 Jordan announced that she would not be a candidate for reelection the following year. In 1979 she became a professor at the Lyndon B. Johnson School of Public Affairs at the University of Texas in Austin.

For further reading:

Bryant, Ira B. *Barbara Charline Jordan: From the Ghetto to the Capitol.* Houston: D. Armstrong Co., Inc., 1977.

Haskins, James. *Barbara Jordan.* New York: The Dial Press, 1977.

Jordan, Barbara, and Shelby Hearon. *Barbara Jordan: A Self-Portrait.* Garden City, N.Y.: Doubleday, 1979.

JOHN MERCER LANGSTON

(Library of Congress)

United States Representative
Republican of Virginia
Fifty-first Congress

The only black representative from Virginia, John Mercer Langston—attorney, public official, educator, author and orator —was a prominent figure long before he served in Congress. He was born in Louisa, Virginia, on December 14, 1829. His father, Ralph Quarles, was a plantation owner; his mother, Lucy Langston, was a free black. Upon the death of both parents in 1834 he was sent by the executors of his father's estate to live with a family friend in Chillicothe, Ohio. In August 1849 Langston received a B.A. from Oberlin College and received an M.A. from the same institution three years later. Denied admission to two law schools because of his race, he read law with Judge Philemon Bliss in Elyria, Ohio. In September 1854 he was admitted to the Ohio bar and commenced practice in Brownhelm. The next month he married Caroline Wall, who also attended Oberlin Col-

73

lege. On April 2, 1855, he was elected clerk of Brownhelm township on the Liberty Party ticket—becoming perhaps the first black elected to public office in the United States.

In 1856 Langston moved from Brownhelm to Oberlin and four years later was elected to its board of education. During the Civil War he worked as an agent recruiting black soldiers in the Midwest. In 1864 he was elected leader of the National Equal Rights League and advocated black suffrage. Immediately following the war he served on the Oberlin City Council and was again a member of the Oberlin Board of Education. In 1867 Langston became inspector general of the Freedmen's Bureau and toured the South encouraging freedmen to seek educational opportunities for themselves and their children. Shortly thereafter he founded and organized the law department of the newly formed Howard University in Washington, serving as its dean from 1868 to 1875.

Langston moved his family from Oberlin to the nation's capital in 1871; the same year he accepted an appointment from President Grant (for whom he had campaigned in 1868) as a member of the District of Columbia Board of Health. In 1874 and 1875 he served as vice president and acting president of Howard. He resigned as vice president and law school dean after the board of trustees denied his bid for appointment to a full term as president of the university.

President Hayes appointed Langston in 1877 as resident minister to Haiti and chargé d'affaires in Santo Domingo. After giving up his posts in 1885, Langston petitioned the Court of Claims to recover $7,666 in salary withheld from him after diplomatic salaries were reduced by the House Appropriations Committee. In 1886 the Supreme Court ruled in his favor. In late 1885 Langston assumed the presidency of the Virginia Normal and Collegiate Institute in Petersburg and served until 1887 when control of the Institute's board of visitors passed into Democratic hands.

In 1888 Langston ran for the House of Representatives from Virginia's Fourth Congressional District. Denied the Republican nomination, he ran as an independent, and initial results indicated that he lost by 641 votes to the Democratic candidate, Edward C. Venable, in an election marred by charges of fraud and intimidation. Langston challenged the results and on September 23, 1890, the House, with virtually all Democratic members refusing to appear, declared him the winner of the contest and seated him in Venable's place for the remainder of the Fifty-first Congress. House Democrats boycotted his swearing-in ceremony.

Langston had only a week to take up his duties before returning to his district to campaign for reelection. Democrat James Epes defeated him by about 3,000 votes. Again Langston believed that he had been deprived of victory by fraud, but an appeal to the House would be futile since the 1890 elections had given the Democrats a 138-seat majority.

Returning to the capital for the opening of the second session in December, Langston served on the Committee on Education and tried unsuccessfully to establish a national industrial university for black citizens. He advocated the observance of Lincoln's and Grant's birthdays as national holidays and spoke in favor of the Voting Rights Act of 1870. He also called for the rehabilitation of the United States Merchant Marine. Langston attempted to appoint black applicants to the United States Naval Academy, but Navy secretary Benjamin Tracy did not act on the matter. On March 3, 1891, Langston's congressional career came to an end.

In 1892, Fourth District Republicans asked Langston to run again for Congress, but he declined, telling them that Republicans were more likely to win in the district with a white candidate. He spent his remaining years in Petersburg and Washington, keeping in touch with politics and working on his autobiography, *From the Virginia Plantation to the National Capitol*, published in 1894. Langston died at his Washington home on November 15, 1897.

For further reading:

Cheek, William F. "A Negro Runs For Congress: John Mercer Langston and the Virginia Campaign of 1888." *Journal of Negro History* 52 (January 1967): pp. 14-34.

Cheek, William F., and Aimee Lee Cheek. *John Mercer Langston and the Fight for Black Freedom, 1829-65.* Urbana: University of Illinois Press, 1989.

Foner, Philip S. "The First Publicly-Elected Black Official in the United States Reports His Election." *Negro History Bulletin* 37 (April/May 1974): p. 237.

Langston, John Mercer. *From the Virginia Plantation to the National Capitol,* 1894. Reprint. New York: Arno Press, 1969.

GEORGE THOMAS (MICKEY) LELAND

(Office of Representative Leland)

United States Representative
Democrat of Texas
Ninety-sixth—One Hundred First Congresses

In his six terms as a representative from Texas, Mickey Leland emerged as a national spokesman for the problems of hunger in the United States and throughout the world. As chairman of the Select Committee on Hunger and in numerous visits to famine-stricken regions of Africa, he drew attention to the severe malnutrition and starvation among refugees in Sudan and Ethiopia and helped secure congressional approval of relief efforts for that region.

George Thomas "Mickey" Leland was born November 27, 1944, in Lubbock, Texas, and grew up in Houston. In 1970 he received a B.S. degree in pharmacy from Texas Southern University in Houston and was an instructor of clinical pharmacy at the same school. As a student he also was involved in the civil rights movement.

Leland first ran for public office in 1972 when he won election as a representative to the Texas state legislature. He also became involved with party politics as a member of the Democratic National Committee from 1976 to 1985. He served as a delegate to the Texas Constitutional Convention in 1974.

Barbara Jordan's surprise decision not to seek reelection in 1978 offered Mickey Leland an opportunity to move from the Texas legislature to the U.S. Congress. After winning a plurality in the Democratic primary of 1978, Leland won the runoff and in November succeeded Jordan as representative from the Eighteenth District of Texas.

In his first term in Congress Leland received a valuable seat on the Interstate and Foreign Commerce (later Energy and Commerce) Committee where he served throughout his term. He also served on the Post Office and Civil Service Committee and was chairman of the Subcommittee on Postal Operations and Services. Leland served on the Committee on the District of Columbia in the Ninety-sixth through Ninety-ninth Congresses. Leland was instrumental in establishing the Select Committee on Hunger in 1984 and served as chairman through the remainder of his term.

In addition to his regular committee responsibilities, Leland was chairman of the Congressional Black Caucus for the Ninety-ninth Congress. During his tenure he successfully urged passage of stronger sanctions against the South African government.

In the summer of 1989, Leland, as he often had before, traveled to Ethiopia to visit a United Nations refugee camp. On August 7 a plane carrying Leland, congressional staff members, State Department officials, and Ethiopian escorts crashed in a mountainous region near Gambela, Ethiopia, killing all on board.

JOHN R. LEWIS

(Office of Representative Lewis)

United States Representative
Democrat of Georgia
One Hundredth—One Hundred First Congresses

Before his election to the House of Representatives in 1986, John Lewis was best known as one of the founders and chairmen of the Student Non-Violent Coordinating Committee. While chairman of SNCC, Lewis helped Martin Luther King, Jr., organize the march in 1965 from Selma to Montgomery, Alabama, in protest of the continued denial of voting rights. He remained active in the campaign for black voter registration and anti-poverty programs before entering local politics in the 1980s.

Lewis was born February 21, 1940, in Troy, Alabama, and grew up on his family's farm. He attended the American Baptist Theological Seminary in Nashville where he received a B.A. in 1961 before entering Fisk University in the same city. Lewis joined with other students in Nashville to organize sit-in demonstrations at segregated lunch counters in the

79

city. Following their repeated arrests, Lewis and other students realized the need to organize their own efforts and the protests of other students across the South, and thus established the Student Non-Violent Coordinating Committee.

Although only in his early twenties, Lewis became a recognized leader of the civil rights movement because of his involvement with the "freedom rides" to challenge segregation in bus terminals, his speech at the March on Washington in 1963 and his organization of the "Mississippi Freedom Summer" in 1964 and other voter registration campaigns in the South. Lewis remained chairman of SNCC until 1966 when members of the organization rejected his emphasis on nonviolence and elected Stokely Carmichael to succeed him.

Lewis remained active in the civil rights movement through his work in directing the Field Foundation's welfare and civil rights programs and his association with welfare and voter registration programs of the Southern Regional Council. He directed the Voter Education Project that helped to register over four million blacks.

Lewis's first venture into elective politics came in 1977 when he ran in the special election to fill the vacancy left when Andrew Young resigned from the House of Representatives to serve as Ambassador to the United Nations. Lewis lost the seat to Wyche Fowler, but later that year received an appointment as a director of ACTION, the federal volunteer agency, under President Jimmy Carter. In 1980 he resigned from the federal government and became community affairs director of the National Consumer Co-op Bank in Atlanta. He first won election to the Atlanta City Council in 1981 and served until June of 1986 when he ran for Congress.

In the Democratic primary for the seat left vacant by Wyche Fowler's run for the Senate, Lewis faced another veteran of the civil-rights movement, Julian Bond. Lewis won the hard-fought campaign and easily defeated his Republican opponent in the fall. In 1988 he won reelection to the One Hundred First Congress. He serves on the Committee on Interior and Insular Affairs and the Committee on Public Works and Transportation.

JEFFERSON FRANKLIN LONG

(Library of Congress)

United States Representative
Republican of Georgia
Forty-first Congress

The first black Member to speak on the floor of the House of Representatives, Jefferson Franklin Long, was for a century the only black representative from Georgia and had the shortest term of office of any black member of Congress. He was born a slave in Knoxville in the black belt of west central Georgia on March 3, 1836. The story of his early years is uncertain. By the end of the Civil War Long had received an education and was working as a tailor in Macon.

Long's prosperous business gave him the financial freedom to pursue a political career. By 1867 he was active in the Georgia Educational Association, a body formed to protect and advance the interests of freedmen. Long soon achieved prominence as he traveled the state for the Republican Party, organizing local branches and encouraging black voter registration. He served on the state Republican central committee and was chairman of an October 1869 convention at Macon on problems faced by freedmen. The meeting proposed the establishment of a public school system and urged improved working conditions for black laborers and tenant farmers.

Congress delayed Georgia's readmission to the Union after a coalition of white Republicans and Conservatives expelled twenty-eight black members from the Georgia legislature in 1868. Not until the black legislators returned to their seats and the state legislature ratified the Fifteenth Amendment did Congress accept Georgia's readmission.

In December 1870 Georgia held elections for two sets of representatives—one for the third and last session of the Forty-first Congress and one for the Forty-second Congress, which would convene in March 1871. Most Republican district conventions named black candidates to run for the abbreviated term in the Forty-first Congress while choosing whites to stand for election to the full term to begin the following March. In the Fourth Congressional District, Long was chosen to contest the seat for the Forty-first Congress while a white state senator, Thomas Jefferson Speer, was slated to run for the Forty-second Congress. Long was elected and was sworn in on January 16, 1871.

On February 1, 1871, Long delivered the first speech by a black representative on the floor of Congress. He spoke in opposition to a bill that would have altered the oath required of former Confederates seeking a restoration of their political rights. Long believed that this measure would only be of help to members of secret intimidation societies who committed acts of racial violence. He pointed to grievous conditions in Georgia—the nighttime murders of those loyal to the Reconstruction government, men fired from their jobs for carrying the stars and stripes in the streets, the public beating of a federal postmaster—and asked if those responsible for these crimes should be able to take advantage of a modified oath and qualify for public office. Long's effort was in vain. On the same day the bill was approved by the House, 118 to 90, and two weeks later President Grant allowed it to become law without his signature.

Less than a month after his speech, Long's term in office expired. Returning to Georgia, he continued to campaign for Republicans and on election day, 1872, addressed a large gathering of Macon blacks who then marched to the polls and were met by angry armed whites. A brief riot broke out, probably instigated by Democrats wanting to "redeem" Macon and Bibb County from the Reconstruction government. Long was unharmed, but four people were killed. Most black voters left the polls without casting their ballots.

Long and other prominent black Republicans soon became frustrated with the failure of the party's white leadership to treat its black members fairly. During the late 1870s he advised blacks to declare their political independence by supporting independent Democrats, if Republican candidates were unsatisfactory. As blacks began to play less and less of a role in the party's organization, Long's disillusionment with politics deepened. After the mid-1880s he devoted most of his time to his business in Macon, where he died on February 4, 1901.

For further reading:

Matthews, John M. "Jefferson Franklin Long: The Public Career of Georgia's First Black Congressman." *Phylon* 42 (June 1981): pp. 145–156.

JOHN ROY LYNCH

United States Representative
Republican of Mississippi
Forty-third, Forty-fourth, Forty-seventh Congresses

John Roy Lynch was for over a century the only black representative from Mississippi and a man who led a remarkable and varied life of ninety-two years. He was born a slave on Tacony plantation near Vadalia in Concordia Parish, Louisiana, on September 10, 1847. Lynch's father, the plantation's manager, died in April 1849, before completing arrangements to purchase his wife and three sons. His wishes that they be manumitted were ignored, and the family was sold to another planter who moved them to Natchez, Mississippi. After his emancipation in 1863 Lynch became a photographer and by 1866 was manager of a Natchez studio, securing an education at a night school for blacks. He was soon prosperous enough to invest in local real estate. Lynch began to participate in Republican politics, and in April 1869 Governor Adelbert Ames appointed him a justice of the peace.

Lynch was elected to the state house of representatives in November 1869. In January 1872 he was chosen speaker and used this powerful position to apportion Mississippi's six districts into five safe seats for Republicans. The same year Lynch won a seat in Congress from the Sixth District, defeating the incumbent representative, Legrand W. Perce, for the Republican nomination and winning easily over Democrat Hiram Cassidy in the general election.

The twenty-five year old Lynch became a member of the Forty-third Congress on March 4, 1873, and served on the Committee on Mines and Mining and the Committee on Expenditures in the Interior Department. He spoke and worked for House passage of the Civil Rights Act of 1875, pointing out that its enforcement provisions were unrelated to the issue of social equality and only guaranteed to blacks the rights that were already codified in the Fourteenth and Fifteenth Amendments to the Constitution. Lynch also paid close attention to the interests of his constituents. He introduced legislation to donate the Natchez Marine Hospital to the state of Mississippi, to improve navigation on the Pascagoula River, and to reimburse depositors of the failed Freedmen's Savings and Trust Company.

Lynch returned to Mississippi in the spring of 1875 to confront a serious threat to Reconstruction. Democrats there were implementing a "Mississippi Plan" of economic coercion and violence to eliminate black voters and the Republican Party as factors in state politics. Governor Ames vainly asked for federal troops to keep the peace. A conspicuous supporter of the civil rights bill, Lynch was targeted for defeat but won a narrow reelection victory over the Democratic candidate, Roderick Seal. Many Republican voters stayed away from the polls as the Democrats took over state offices. Lynch attacked the activities of the White League and other illegal groups that provoked violent attacks on blacks. On the House floor he consistently defended the administrations of Republican governors Ames and James L. Alcorn against criticism from southern Democrats who claimed that Republican government in Mississippi fostered corruption.

In 1876 Lynch was defeated for reelection by Democrat James R. Chalmers, a former Confederate general and cavalry commander. The House refused to hear Lynch's contest of Chalmers' victory. During the second and last session of the Forty-fourth Congress he accused state Democrats of taking illegal steps to prevent blacks from casting ballots, thereby stealing Mississippi's eight electoral votes from Republican presidential candidate Rutherford B. Hayes.

Although Lynch lost an 1880 congressional bid against Chalmers, he successfully appealed the decision to the House and was seated as a member of the Forty-seventh Congress on April 29, 1882. He sat on the Committee on Education and Labor and the Committee on the Militia. He sponsored legislation to divide Mississippi into two judicial districts and to reimburse the Protestant Orphan Asylum in Natchez $10,000 for damage caused by Union forces during the Civil War. Recalling the yellow fever epidemic of 1878 that had ravaged Memphis and New Orleans, he spoke in favor of an appropriation for the National Board of Health. Lynch spent little time in the Forty-seventh Congress, for it adjourned in early August in anticipation of the midterm election campaign. Democrat Henry S. Van Eaton, a Confederate veteran, defeated Lynch by 900 votes in his reelection bid.

Although his congressional career had ended, Lynch remained deeply involved in political life. In 1884 and 1886 he attempted to regain his seat in the House but lost on both tries. From 1881 to 1892 he was chairman of the Republican state executive committee and was a member of the Republican National Committee from Mississippi from 1884 to 1889. When the Republican National Convention met in Chicago in 1884, Lynch was temporary chairman and delivered the keynote address, the first black ever to do so. He refused an offer of appointment as a special public lands agent from the Cleveland administration, but was fourth auditor of the treasury for the Navy Department under President

Harrison from 1889 to 1893. Lynch was admitted to the Mississippi bar in 1896, opened a Washington law office in 1897 and practiced until the following year, when he was appointed by President McKinley major and additional paymaster of volunteers during the Spanish-American war. He received a presidential appointment as a paymaster in the regular army with the rank of captain in 1901. He was promoted to major in 1906 and retired from the regular army in 1911.

In August 1911 Lynch, who had been divorced in 1900, married the former Cora Williamson. The following year they moved to Chicago where Lynch continued the practice of law. In 1913 he published *The Facts of Reconstruction,* an account of his participation in the politics of post-Civil War Mississippi and a defense of reconstruction. In 1917 and 1918 he published in the *Journal of Negro History* two articles that challenged statements made by historian James Ford Rhodes. In 1922 these articles were published in book form as *Some Historical Errors of James Ford Rhodes.* During the late 1930s he completed his autobiography, *Reminiscences of An Active Life,* but it was not published until 1970. Lynch died in Chicago on November 2, 1939.

For further reading:

Bell, Frank C. "The Life and Times of John R. Lynch: A Case Study 1847-1939." *Journal of Mississippi History* 38 (February 1976): pp. 53-67.

Franklin, John Hope. "John Roy Lynch: Republican Stalwart from Mississippi." In *Southern Black Leaders of the Reconstruction Era,* edited by Howard N. Rabinowitz, pp. 39-58. Urbana: University of Illinois Press, 1982.

Lynch, John Roy. *Reminiscences of an Active Life.* Edited and with an Introduction by John Hope Franklin. Chicago: The University of Chicago Press, 1970.

Mann, Kenneth Eugene. "John Roy Lynch: U.S. Congressman from Mississippi." *Negro History Bulletin* 37 (April/May 1974): pp. 238-241.

RALPH HAROLD METCALFE

United States Representative
Democrat of Illinois
Ninety-second—Ninety-fifth Congresses

Ralph Metcalfe achieved worldwide fame as an athlete before he became a politician and a symbol of independence from the Democratic machine for Chicago's blacks. He was born in Atlanta on May 29, 1910, and moved with his family to Chicago, where he attended public schools. He received a Ph.B. from Marquette University in 1936 and an M.A. in physical education from the University of Southern California in 1939. A competitor in track events since the age of fifteen, he was a medal winner in the Olympics of 1932 and 1936 and coached the track team while teaching political science at Xavier University in New Orleans for six years. He entered the United States Army Transportation Corps in 1942 and was discharged in 1945 as a first lieutenant. The same year he became director of the Chicago Commission on Human Relations' civil rights department and was Illinois State

Athletic Commissioner from 1949 to 1952. In 1952 he was elected Third Ward Democratic Committeeman and won a seat on the Chicago City Council in 1955.

When the powerful but aging First District Representative William L. Dawson, a longtime member of the Democratic machine, decided to retire from the House, he supported Metcalfe, who was elected easily a few days before Dawson's death in November 1970. Metcalfe entered the House on January 3, 1971, and served on the Committee on Merchant Marine and Fisheries and on the Interstate and Foreign Commerce Committee.

A former chairman of the Chicago City Council's housing committee, Metcalfe worked to expand the availability of home improvement loans and federal housing programs and to improve the safety of residents in public housing projects. He also fought to eliminate the practice of "redlining"—the withholding of home-loan funds and insurance from low-income neighborhoods. In an effort to improve the climate for minority-owned businesses, Metcalfe successfully added an amendment to railroad legislation to offer minority firms access to work on projects to revitalize the nation's railroads. As chairman of the Merchant Marine and Fisheries Subcommittee on the Panama Canal, he advocated increased opportunities for education, housing and jobs in the Canal Zone, and favored passage of the Panama Canal treaty ratified in April 1978. Metcalfe also held hearings that publicized deficiencies in federal programs and guidelines for airline safety, prison administration and preventive medical care for schoolchildren.

In 1972 Metcalfe broke with Chicago's Democratic machine over the issue of police brutality in the black community. Charging that blacks had been mistreated and abused by the police department, he conducted public hearings to give victims and witnesses a forum and organized a citizens' group to lobby the city government for reforms. He also supported independent anti-machine candidates and refused to endorse Mayor Richard J. Daley in the 1975 mayoral contest. Daley retaliated by depriving Metcalfe of Third Ward patronage and arranging a challenge in the 1976 Democratic primary. Metcalfe decisively defeated Daley aide Erwin A. France and was unopposed for renomination in 1978. He died on October 10, 1978, only a month before his almost certain reelection to a fifth term.

KWEISI MFUME

(Office of Representative Mfume)

United States Representative
Democrat of Maryland
One Hundredth—One Hundred First Congresses

Kweisi Mfume's political success stands in sharp contrast to his youth in the inner city of Baltimore where he was born October 24, 1948. After the death of his mother and the scattering of his family, Mfume overcame a troubled youth and economic hardship before making a successful return to high school and graduation from Morgan State University in 1976 with a Bachelor of Urban Planning degree. He received a M.A. degree from Johns Hopkins University in 1984. He was a member of Morgan State's faculty, teaching political science and communications, as well as serving as program director of the University's radio station, WEAA-FM.

Raised as Frizzell Gray, Mfume adopted his African name ("conquering son of kings") and was elected in 1979 to the Baltimore City Council, where he chaired the health subcommittee of Baltimore City and served until his election to Congress. While on the city council he successfully sponsored legislation requiring Baltimore to divest itself of investments in companies doing business in South Africa. A member of the Maryland Democratic state central committee for the Fortieth Legislative District, he also was elected a delegate to the Democratic National Conventions of 1980, 1984 and 1988 as a delegate from the Seventh Congressional District. Mfume was Baltimore co-chair of Senator Edward Kennedy's presidential campaign in 1980 and served as Maryland co-chair of the 1984 and 1988 campaigns of the Reverend Jesse Jackson.

After Seventh Congressional District Representative Parren J. Mitchell announced his retirement from Congress in 1985, Mfume defeated a crowded field in the September 1986 primary and easily won the general election. As a member of the One Hundredth and One Hundred First Congresses, Mfume serves on the Banking, Finance and Urban Affairs Committee and three of its subcommittees (Housing and Community Development, Economic Stabilization, and International Development); the Small Business Committee and two of its subcommittees (Minority Enterprise, and Exports, Tourism and Special Problems); and the Select Committee on Hunger. During the One Hundredth Congress (1987–1989), he served as treasurer of the Congressional Black Caucus and in the One Hundred First Congress served as its vice chairman.

THOMAS EZEKIEL MILLER

(Moorland-Spingarn Research Center, Howard University)

United States Representative
Republican of South Carolina
Fifty-first Congress

Thomas Ezekiel Miller was, with the exception of John R. Lynch of Mississippi, the last survivor of the post-Civil War generation of black representatives. The son of a free black couple, he was born on June 17, 1849, in Ferrebeeville, South Carolina, a town named after his mother's family. In 1851 his family moved to Charleston, where Thomas attended black schools. When the Civil War ended Miller journeyed to Hudson, New York, where he worked as a newsboy on a railroad. A scholarship allowed him to enter Lincoln University in Chester County, Pennsylvania, and he graduated in 1872.

In 1872 Miller was school commissioner of Beaufort County, South Carolina. He subsequently moved to Columbia and studied law at the recently integrated University of South Carolina. He also studied with the state solicitor and state supreme court justice. He was admitted to the bar in December 1875. Miller was a member of the state general assembly from 1874 to 1880, when he went to the state senate. The same year he was nominated for lieutenant governor but did not enter the race because the South Carolina Republican Party declined to put forward a state ticket. Miller returned to the state house of representatives in 1877. He served on the Republican state executive committee from 1878 to 1880 and was state party chairman in 1884.

In 1888 Miller ran for Congress from the Seventh District against Democratic candidate William Elliott, who was declared the winner. Miller contested the election, alleging that many black voters who were properly registered had not been permitted to cast their ballots. The House Committee on Elections eventually ruled in his favor, and Miller was sworn into the Fifty-first Congress on September 24, 1890. He took a seat on the Committee on the Library of Congress, but found himself involved in two lengthy contested election cases that diverted his attention from legislative business.

In 1890 Miller ran for reelection and was the apparent victor over Elliott and independent Republican E.W. Brayton. Elliott insisted that the vote count was fraudulent and challenged the results. The South Carolina Supreme Court ruled that Elliott was entitled to the seat because the color and size of Miller's ballots were illegal. When the Fifty-second Congress assembled on December 7, 1891, Miller asked the House to declare him the rightful winner, but a majority of the Elections Committee in February 1893 gave the seat to Elliott. By the time of the committee's ruling, Miller had been defeated for the Republican nomination by George W. Murray, who was elected to represent the Seventh District in the Fifty-third Congress.

Miller had lost his reelection bid to the Fifty-third Congress and was challenging Elliott's election to the Fifty-second when he spoke to the House in January 1891 on Representative Henry Cabot Lodge's bill authorizing the government to oversee federal elections and protect voters from violence and intimidation. Miller ignored threats that his remarks would endanger his chances of being seated in the next Congress and urged the Senate to follow the House and take favorable action on Lodge's proposal. He rejected Democratic claims that the election law was a "force bill" designed to perpetuate misrule by incompetent and corrupt blacks. On February 14, 1891, Miller delivered a major address in reply to a speech by Senator Alfred H. Colquitt of Georgia, who blamed blacks for retarding the South's economic development. Miller replied that the Colquitt speech was an offensive mixture of theology and political economy that contained groundless slanders against black Americans. White southerners, Miller declared, were chiefly responsible for the region's economic problems because they were motivated by bigotry and vengefulness in denying blacks the full rights of citizenship.

From 1894 to 1896 Miller served once more in the state house of representatives. He was a delegate in 1895 to the state constitutional convention that disfranchised most blacks by approving election laws requiring, among other things, that voters read and write any part of the South Carolina constitution or prove that they owned at least $300 in property. Miller, Congressman Murray and former Representative Robert Smalls spoke against these and other racist provisions, but their efforts were unsuccessful.

After Claflin College in Orangeburg lost its federal funding, Miller helped establish the State Negro College (now South Carolina State College) in the same town. In March 1896 he became the college's president and worked to promote the employment of black teachers in black public schools. He was forced to resign in 1911 by Governor Coleman L. Blease, whom he had opposed in the previous year's election. Miller retired from active pursuits and lived in Charleston until 1923, when he moved to Philadelphia. He returned to Charleston in 1934 and died there on April 8, 1938.

ARTHUR WERGS MITCHELL

(Library of Congress)

United States Representative
Democrat of Illinois
Seventy-fourth—Seventy-seventh Congresses

Arthur Mitchell, born on a farm near Lafayette, Alabama, on December 22, 1883, was the first black representative elected as a Democrat. He attended public schools and entered Tuskegee Institute in 1897, working his way through as a farm laborer and as an office boy for Booker T. Washington. He taught in rural schools in Georgia and Alabama and attempted to put Washington's ideas on farm management and land ownership into practice by founding and serving ten years as president of the Armstrong Agricultural School in West Butler, Alabama. He studied law, was admitted to the bar in 1927 and began practicing in Washington, D.C., before moving to Chicago in 1929. He continued the practice of law in Chicago and also engaged in the real estate business.

Mitchell entered political life as a Republican, but like many black Americans, he shifted his allegiance to the Democratic Party in the early days of the New Deal. In 1934 he sought the Democratic nomination for Congress from the First District, but was defeated by Harry Baker. When Baker died before the general election, party leaders in the district selected Mitchell as the nominee. In a campaign against venerable Republican Congressman Oscar De Priest, Mitchell succeeded in turning the contest into a referendum on the public relief policies of President Roosevelt. Mitchell was elected and took his seat in the Seventy-fourth Congress on January 3, 1935. He served on the Committee on Post Offices and Post Roads, a position he would retain throughout his eight years in the House.

In October 1935 Mitchell denounced the Italian invasion of Ethiopia, condemning the Mussolini regime for its exploitation of a weaker nation. Like his predecessor, De Priest, he nominated black youths as candidates for United States military academies. In 1936 Mitchell gave a seconding speech for Roosevelt's renomination at the Democratic convention and served as western director of minority affairs for the president's reelection campaign. Noting that blacks had been victimized over the years by unfavorable Supreme Court rulings, he wholeheartedly supported Roosevelt's controversial plan to reorganize the federal judiciary in 1937. Mitchell charged that the Court had often used the Fourteenth Amendment to protect large corporations and property holders instead of employing it for its intended purpose of defending the citizenship rights of blacks.

In April 1937 Mitchell travelled from Chicago to Hot Springs, Arkansas, on the Chicago, Rock Island and Pacific Railway. When the train crossed into Arkansas, a conductor forced Mitchell out of the Pullman car for which he had bought two first class tickets. The Congressman rode the rest of the journey in a decrepit "Jim Crow" car. Mitchell then followed in the footsteps of another black representative, James E. O'Hara, and challenged transport segregation. He sued the railroad and filed a complaint with the Interstate Commerce Commission, arguing that interstate trains should be exempt from the Arkansas law requiring "separate but equal" train accommodations. After his complaint was dismissed by the I.C.C. and a Federal District court, Mitchell argued his case before the Supreme Court. In April 1941 the court unanimously held, in *Mitchell* vs. *United States et al.*, that black passengers had the right to receive the same accommodations and treatment as did whites. Mitchell hailed the decision as a positive step forward, but it was not until 1955 that the I.C.C. prohibited segregation on interstate travel in trains, buses and in the public waiting rooms of railroad and bus stations.

Throughout his congressional career Mitchell submitted bills to hold state and local officials accountable for lynching and to outlaw racial discrimination in the civil service. He attacked several labor unions for agreeing to contracts that excluded blacks from employment. In October 1942 he strongly supported a proposal outlawing the poll tax as a condition for voting. At the opening of the Second World War, he declared that if blacks could be called on to fight for the United States in war they were also entitled to the franchise.

Mitchell did not run for reelection in 1942, telling House colleagues that he preferred to help improve race relations by working outside of Congress with groups that were active in the South. He moved to Petersburg, Virginia, and devoted himself to farming, lecturing and the activities of organizations such as the Southern Regional Council. He died in Petersburg on May 9, 1968.

PARREN JAMES MITCHELL

*United States Representative
Democrat of Maryland
Ninety-Second—Ninety-ninth Congresses*

Parren J. Mitchell, the first black representative from Maryland, was born in Baltimore on April 29, 1922. After graduating from Douglass High School in Baltimore in 1940 he entered the United States Army in 1942, serving as a commissioned officer and company commander with the Ninety-second Infantry Division. Following his discharge in 1946 Mitchell received an A.B. from Morgan State College in 1950 and a M.A. from the University of Maryland in 1952. He was an instructor of sociology at Morgan State during 1953–1954 and supervisor of probation work for the Supreme Bench of Baltimore City from 1954 to 1957. From 1963 to 1965 he was executive secretary of the Maryland Human Relations Commission, overseeing implementation of the state's public accommodations law. Mitchell was director of the Baltimore Community Action Agency, an anti-poverty program, from

1965 to 1968, when he returned to Morgan State as a professor of sociology and assistant director of its Urban Affairs Institute. In 1969 he became president of Baltimore Neighborhoods, Inc.

Mitchell unsuccessfully challenged Seventh District Representative Samuel N. Friedel in the September 1968 Democratic primary, but defeated Friedel in their 1970 rematch and won the general election over Republican Peter Parker. He was sworn in as a member of the Ninety-second Congress on January 3, 1971.

A member of the Committee on the Budget and the Banking, Finance and Urban Affairs Committee, Mitchell became chairman of the Committee on Small Business at the beginning of the Ninety-seventh Congress in 1981. Throughout his congressional career he directed many of his legislative efforts toward promoting minority-owned businesses. He sought passage of legislation requiring a fixed percentage of the contracts for federal projects to be set aside for minority firms. In order to provide small businesses with more opportunities to procure contracts awarded by the Defense Department, he successfully fought to remove department limits on the number of companies permitted to bid for spare parts contracts. Mitchell was a strong supporter of the Small Business Administration and opposed efforts to increase the interest rates for loans to small businesses and to reduce S.B.A. disaster loans. He opposed the establishment of a sub-minimum wage for people aged eighteen and younger, and called for strong sanctions banning all new investment by United States firms in South Africa.

Mitchell announced in September 1985 that he would not seek reelection to a ninth term. He resides in Baltimore, Maryland.

GEORGE WASHINGTON MURRAY

United States Representative
Republican of South Carolina
Fifty-third—Fifty-fourth Congresses

George Washington Murray was a leader in the struggle to protect black voting rights in the post-Reconstruction South. He was born to slave parents near Rembert, Sumter County, South Carolina, on September 22, 1853, and attended public schools, the University of South Carolina and the State Normal Institute at Columbia. After his graduation in 1876 Murray farmed in Sumter County, taught school and worked as a lecturer for the Colored Farmers' Alliance.

Murray participated in local Republican politics and was rewarded for his work for the Harrison-Morton ticket of 1888 with an appointment as inspector of customs at the port of Charleston in February 1890. The same year he ran for the Republican nomination to Congress from the district but lost to E.W. Brayton and former congressman Thomas E.

Miller. In 1892 Murray tried again and defeated Brayton, Miller, and former representative Robert Smalls for the nomination. On the day of the general election, the notorious "eight-ballot box" rule, designed to prevent large numbers of blacks from voting, jeopardized Murray's election. The state board of election canvassers, which contained followers of Governor Benjamin R. Tillman, declared Murray the winner over E.M. Moise, a Democrat who opposed Tillman on economic issues.

Murray took his seat in the Fifty-third Congress on March 4, 1893, and was a member of the Committee on Education. In August he asked in his first House speech that the Sherman Silver Purchase Act not be repealed. He fought unsuccessfully against the Democratic majority's efforts to annul Reconstruction laws designed to safeguard the rights of black voters. The following year he spoke in favor of an appropriation for a federal exhibit at the Cotton States and International Exposition in Atlanta, which could be used to make many people aware of black achievements. To prove his point he provided the House with a partial list of ninety-two patents granted by the government for inventions by black Americans. (Eight of the items were agricultural tools invented by Murray himself). After the death of Frederick Douglass in February 1895, Murray asked that the abolitionist and civil rights leader's remains lie in state in the rotunda of the Capitol, but Speaker Charles F. Crisp of Georgia rejected his request.

In 1894 Murray ran for reelection against William Elliott. His Seventh Congressional District had been gerrymandered into a new district, the First, where the black majority faced numerous obstacles to voter registration. Elliott defeated Murray but the incumbent appealed to the state board of election canvassers, charging that many ballot boxes were not properly inspected and that votes had been counted secretly. The board rejected Murray's appeal, but the House Committee on Elections upheld his challenge. He was finally seated as a member of the Fifty-fourth Congress on June 4, 1896. In addition to his Education Committee assignment, Murray took a seat on the Committee on Expenditures in the Treasury Department.

New threats to black political rights in South Carolina prevented Murray from attending many meetings of the third session of the Fifty-third Congress in the first months of 1895. Followers of Governor Tillman had passed a state referendum authorizing a convention to revise the Constitution of 1868 and disfranchise blacks. At a Republican party conference and at meetings throughout South Carolina, Murray organized blacks to register to vote for delegates to the state convention. He also raised money to pay for legal counsel to challenge the new registration laws in federal court. Only six blacks were chosen as delegates to an overwhelmingly white convention that devised requirements for residency, poll taxes, property ownership and literacy that effectively deprived South Carolina's black citizens of the right to vote. Legal efforts to reverse the trend faced an 1898 Supreme Court ruling that poll taxes did not violate the Fourteenth Amendment.

A division between the "Black and Tan" and "Lily White" factions of the state Republican Party threatened Murray's already dim prospects for reelection. By election day, November 3, 1896, black voter registration had been so circumscribed that Elliott was able to win handily. Murray announced that he would challenge the validity of the nine Democratic electoral votes South Carolina cast in the presidential contest unless Congress investigated the state's election laws. Influential Republican congressmen urged him to abandon this plan in order not to jeopardize William McKinley's chances for the presidency. Murray agreed, but he continued to press for a federal investigation of South Carolina politics. Congress adjourned in March 1897, however, without taking action.

After the loss of his House seat Murray resumed farming and invested in tracts of land that were resold to black tenant farmers. In 1905 a circuit court convicted him of forgery as the result of a contract dispute with two tenants. Murray left South Carolina for Chicago to avoid a sentence of three years' hard labor. In Chicago Murray remained active in the local Republican party and wrote two books on race relations: *Race Ideals: Effects,*

Cause and Remedy for the Afro-American Race Troubles (1914); and *Light in Dark Places* (1925). He died in Chicago on April 21, 1926.

For further reading:

Gaboury, William J. "George Washington Murray and the Fight For Political Democracy in South Carolina." *Journal of Negro History* 62 (July 1977): pp. 258–269.

CHARLES EDMUND NASH

(Moorland-Spingarn Research Center, Howard University)

United States Representative
Republican of Louisiana
Forty-fourth Congress

Louisiana's only black representative, Charles Edmund Nash, was born in Opelousas, St. Landry Parish, Louisiana, on May 23, 1844. After attending common schools, he was a bricklayer in New Orleans before enlisting as a private in Company A of the Eighty-second Regiment, United States Volunteers in July 1863. He was later promoted to sergeant major. During the last infantry battle of the war at Fort Blakely, Alabama, on April 9, 1865, he was severely wounded and lost part of his right leg, a disability which often limited his ability to earn a living.

In 1869 Nash was appointed night inspector in the New Orleans Custom House, an important source of federal patronage in Louisiana. Local Republicans apparently concluded that Nash's background of heroic wartime service and loyal party work made him an attractive candidate for public office. In 1874 he

101

was elected to the House from the Sixth Congressional District. Unlike many black members of Reconstruction-era Congresses, Nash faced no challenges to his election and seating. Assigned to the Committee on Education and Labor, Nash was present when the first session of the Forty-fourth Congress convened on December 6, 1875.

Nash possessed neither the seniority nor rhetorical ability to wield much influence during his brief congressional term. On February 28, 1876, he proposed legislation to finance a survey of the Courtableau Bayou, but the measure expired after reaching the Committee on Commerce. Nash often found it difficult to speak on the House floor. In May, he made an unsuccessful effort to talk about a disputed House election in Louisiana's Fifth District. Nash refused to allow his remarks to be placed in an appendix to the *Congressional Record*, insisting that he wanted his words heard by the House and not merely printed. On June 7, he was able to speak to the House on political conditions in the South, praising the Republican Party for what it had done to promote the cause of emancipated freedmen. Nash also called for the enforcement of constitutional provisions designed to protect freedmen and urged southern states to promote public education to forestall the efforts of demagogues to exploit racial prejudice. He concluded by reaffirming his faith in American greatness and in the inevitability of racial progress.

Internal divisions in the Louisiana Republican party hampered Nash's campaign for re-election in 1876. He lost to Democrat Edward Robertson by 4,300 votes. The outcome of his campaign was overshadowed by the explosive issue of disputed Louisiana returns in the Hayes-Tilden presidential contest. After leaving Congress, Nash never held elective office. He returned to the bricklayer's trade and served as postmaster at Washington in St. Landry parish briefly in 1882. Age and the effects of war injuries forced Nash to abandon his trade, and he later worked as a cigar maker. He died in New Orleans on June 21, 1913.

ROBERT NELSON CORNELIUS NIX, Sr.

(Library of Congress)

United States Representative
Democrat of Pennsylvania
Eighty-fifth—Ninety-fifth Congresses

Robert N.C. Nix, the first black representative from Pennsylvania, was born on August 9, 1905, in Orangeburg, South Carolina, where his father, Nelson, was dean of South Carolina State College. After graduation from Townsend Harris High School in New York City, Nix entered Lincoln University in Chester County, Pennsylvania, and graduated in 1921. He received his law degree from the University of Pennsylvania law school in 1924 and began practice in Philadelphia the following year. He became active in Democratic politics and was elected a committeeman from the Forty-fourth Ward in 1932. From 1934 to 1938 he worked for the Commonwealth of Pennsylvania as a special deputy attorney general in the revenue department and as a special assistant deputy attorney general.

After Representative Earl Chudoff resigned his congressional seat to become a Philadelphia judge, Nix defeated two opponents in a special election to fill the vacancy and was sworn in as a member of the Eighty-sixth Congress on May 20, 1958. For the next two decades he withstood opponents' charges of absenteeism and of blind allegiance to Philadelphia's Democratic machine, eventually becoming the second most senior black representative.

During his years in the House Nix served on the Veterans' Affairs Committee, Foreign Affairs Committee, and the Committee on Merchant Marine and Fisheries. In 1977, after fourteen years as a member, he became chairman of the Committee on the Post Office and Civil Service. A politician who rarely sought or attracted widespread publicity, Nix was generally loyal to the Kennedy and Johnson administrations and supported much liberal legislation. He sponsored bills to preserve the Philadelphia navy yard and to establish a "senior service corps" that would employ people over sixty years of age. Disturbed by rumors that the March on Washington scheduled for August 1963 might result in rioting and violence, Nix told the House of his faith that the marchers' campaign to secure equal rights for minorities would be carried out peacefully. He worked for passage of the landmark civil rights legislation of the 1960s and privately sought to prevent the House from denying Representative Adam Clayton Powell, Jr., his seat in the Ninetieth Congress. In 1975, as chairman of the Subcommittee on International Economic Policy, Nix led an investigation of the use of funds by defense contractors to pay foreign consultants, agents, governmental officials and political parties. Nix later introduced an amendment to the Foreign Military Sales Act requiring the Defense Department to provide Congress with information on the identities of and fees received by agents who negotiate arms sales transactions for American firms.

In 1976 Nix barely survived a primary challenge from William H. Gray III, and two years later he lost to Gray in an effort to win nomination to an eleventh term. Nix remained leader of the Thirty-second Ward until his death in Philadelphia on June 22, 1987.

JAMES EDWARD O'HARA

(Moorland-Spingarn Research Center, Howard University)

United States Representative
Republican of North Carolina
Forty-eighth—Forty-ninth Congresses

The son of an Irish merchant and a West Indian woman, James Edward O'Hara was born in New York City on February 26, 1844, and attended public schools there. In 1862 O'Hara moved to North Carolina with a group of missionaries and began the study of law. He also attended law classes at Howard University but did not graduate. In June 1871 O'Hara was admitted to the North Carolina bar and subsequently commenced practice in Enfield in Halifax County.

In the years following the Civil War O'Hara often served as a secretary at freedmen's and Republican party meetings, composing reports of these gatherings for newspaper readers. He was a delegate to and engrossing clerk of the 1868 North Carolina Constitutional Convention and served in the state house of representatives in 1868 and 1869. In 1873 he became chairman of the Halifax County board of commissioners. O'Hara was also a delegate from Halifax County to the state convention held in Raleigh during the fall of 1875 which drafted ordinances to amend the constitution of 1868.

O'Hara made his first bid for Congress in 1874 but lost the Second Congressional District's Republican nomination to John A. Hyman. O'Hara received the party's endorsement in 1878 but another Republican, James H. Harris, divided the party's vote, narrowly giving the election to Democrat William H. Kitchin. O'Hara challenged the results, but his evidence was destroyed when his house burned down. He failed to persuade either the state courts or the Forty-sixth Congress to unseat Kitchin. In 1880 O'Hara again campaigned for the Republican nomination in the Second District and lost to Orlando Hubbs. In 1882 he finally won the nomination and the seat by a wide margin over token opposition.

Democrats controlled the Forty-eighth Congress in which O'Hara took his seat on March 4, 1883. Until the arrival of Robert Smalls in March 1884, O'Hara was the only black member of Congress. He served on the Committee on Mines and Mining and the Committee on Expenditures on Public Buildings. Shortly after the beginning of the first session on December 3, 1883, O'Hara proposed a civil rights constitutional amendment, but the House failed to consider it. He was unable to secure passage of legislation to reimburse depositors of the failed Freedmen's Savings and Trust Company for their losses. When the House considered a bill to regulate interstate commerce, O'Hara added an amendment requiring equal accommodations for all travelers on railroad passenger cars regardless of color. O'Hara maintained that Congress had authority over passenger as well as freight cars. If Congress could set standards for the treatment of animals transported by rail, it could also take steps to assure equal treatment of citizens who rode the railroads. The Interstate Commerce Act, however, finally passed by Congress in 1887, fell short of what O'Hara had envisaged, and permitted railroads to segregate passengers.

O'Hara was reelected over Democrat Frederick A. Woodward in 1884 and moved from the Committee on Mines and Mining to the Committee on Invalid Pensions when the Forty-ninth Congress convened in December 1885. In January 1886 he made an unsuccessful effort to reappraise the value of the legendary ship, the *Planter,* made famous by the exploits of Robert Smalls, and to extend the benefits received by Smalls and his crew. When, on March 17, a white mob surrounded and entered the Carrollton, Mississippi, courthouse, where seven whites were about to be tried for assaulting two blacks, and opened fire on all the blacks present, killing eleven and wounding nine, O'Hara introduced a resolution calling on Speaker John G. Carlisle to appoint a committee of five members to investigate the incident and issue a report. The proposal was referred to the Rules Committee but never emerged. The following year O'Hara expressed an interest in women's rights. In January 1887 he amended a District of Columbia appropriations bill by inserting a proviso that no discrimination be made in the salaries of male and female teachers who held the same certificates and performed similar duties.

Internal feuds among the Second District's Republicans ended O'Hara's congressional career. Another black Republican, Israel B. Abbott, entered the 1886 race, and Democrat Furnifold McL. Simmons took advantage of the G.O.P. breach, and won with forty-five percent of the vote. O'Hara never gain held public office. He returned to his law practice in partnership with his son Raphael. He died in New Bern on September 15, 1905.

For further reading:

Anderson, Eric. "James O'Hara of North Carolina: Black Leadership and Local Government." In *Southern Black Leaders of the Reconstruction Era,* edited by Howard N. Rabinowitz, pp. 101-125. Urbana: University of Illinois Press, 1982.

Reid, George W. "Four In Black: North Carolina's Black Congressmen, 1874-1901." *Journal of Negro History* 64 (Summer 1979): pp. 229-243.

MAJOR ROBERT ODELL OWENS

(Office of Representative Owens)

United States Representative
Democrat of New York
Ninety-eighth—One Hundred First Congresses

Major Owens entered Congress in 1983 following an extensive career in both the library system and anti-poverty and community action programs in New York City. Born in Memphis, Tennessee, on June 28, 1936, Owens attended Hamilton High School in Memphis and received a B.A. degree from Morehouse College in 1956. After earning an M.S. degree in library science from Atlanta University in 1957, Owens joined the Brooklyn public library system and in 1964 became its Brownsville Community Coordinator, serving in this capacity until 1966.

During the civil rights movement, Owens became actively involved in politics through his work as chairman of the Brooklyn Congress of Racial Equality from 1964 to 1966, and as vice president of the Metropolitan Council on Housing, a group advocating the rights of tenants throughout New York City.

He joined others in working to reform Brooklyn's Democratic Party, and in 1966 was named executive director of a community renewal organization, the Brownsville Community Council. In March 1968, New York mayor John V. Lindsay appointed Owens New York's Commissioner of Community Development, a community action agency organizing and supervising self-help and anti-poverty programs. Owens remained active in library affairs as adjunct professor of library science and director of the Community Media Program at Columbia University from 1973 to 1975 and as the keynote speaker at the 1979 White House Conference on Libraries.

In 1974, Owens was elected to the New York State Senate, representing the Brownsville and East New York sections of Brooklyn. While serving in Albany he chaired the senate day care task force and was a member of the senate finance and social services committee.

Running as a candidate independent of the Brooklyn Democratic machine, Owens was elected to the House of Representatives from the Twelfth Congressional District of New York in 1982, succeeding Representative Shirley Chisholm, who had retired after seven terms in Congress. He is a member of the Government Operations Committee and is a senior member of the Education and Labor Committee. In 1987 he became chairman of the Subcommittee on Select Education and presided over its hearings on child abuse, family violence and the education of the disabled. Owens has also been interested in educational issues, serving as the chair of the Higher Education Brain Trust of the Congressional Black Caucus. He has focused many of his efforts on restoration of federal funding for the nation's library services and institutions of higher education and for programs to alleviate the problems of high school dropouts, historically black colleges and the black family.

DONALD MILFORD PAYNE

(Office of Representative Payne)

United States Representative
Democrat of New Jersey
One Hundred First Congress

The first black member of Congress from New Jersey, Donald Payne entered the House of Representatives following a career of involvement with New Jersey's city and county politics and with the youth activities and training programs of the Young Men's Christian Association. Born in Newark, New Jersey, on July 16, 1934, Payne received a B.A. degree in social studies from Seton Hall University in 1957 and began his association with the Y.M.C.A., traveling as its representative to more than eighty countries, assisting in the development of education, housing and systems of local government. He was elected the first black president of the Y.M.C.A.'s of the United States in 1970 and chaired the Geneva-based World Y.M.C.A. Refugee and Rehabilitation Committee from 1973 to 1981.

Payne entered public life in 1972, when he was elected to the Essex County Board of Chosen Freeholders, an office he held until 1978. In 1977 his fellow board members chose him as director, with responsibility for the administration of Essex county's operating budget. Payne was a member of the Newark Municipal Council from 1982 until his election to Congress. He also worked as a community relations consultant for an insurance company executive and as vice president of a minority-owned computer forms manufacturer.

In 1980 and 1986 Payne mounted a Democratic primary challenge to Congressman Peter W. Rodino, Jr., who had represented New Jersey's Tenth District since 1949. After Rodino's March 1988 announcement that he would not seek a twenty-first House term, Payne won both the nomination and the general election by large margins. He is currently a member of the Education and Labor Committee, the Foreign Affairs Committee, and the Government Operations Committee.

ADAM CLAYTON POWELL, Jr.

United States Representative
Democrat of New York
Seventy-ninth—Ninetieth, Ninety-first Congresses

Adam Clayton Powell, Jr., was born in New Haven, Connecticut, on November 29, 1908. At the age of six months he moved with his parents to New York City, where his minister father developed the century-old Abyssinian Baptist Church into one of the largest congregations in the United States. After attending public schools and the City College of New York, Powell graduated with a B.A. degree from Colgate University in 1930, and received a M.A. degree in religious education from Columbia University in 1931. While the assistant minister and business manager of the Abyssinian Church in 1930, Powell used picket lines and mass meetings to demand reforms at Harlem Hospital, which had dismissed five black doctors from its staff because of their race. Beginning in 1932, he administered an extensive church-sponsored relief program providing food, clothing and temporary jobs for thousands of Harlem's homeless and unemployed. It was during these Depression years that Powell established himself as a charismatic and successful civil rights leader as he organized mass meetings, rent strikes and public campaigns that forced restaurants, retail stores, bus lines, utilities, telephone companies, Harlem Hospital and the 1939 World's Fair either to hire or to begin promoting black employees. These impressive victories secured for Powell an extraordinarily loyal support from Harlem residents who would stand behind him almost to the very end of his controversial career.

Powell succeeded his father as pastor of Abyssinian Baptist Church in 1936. In 1941 he was elected as an independent to the New York City Council. He was publisher and editor of *The People's Voice,* a weekly newspaper, from 1941 to 1945. In 1942 he became a member of the New York State Office of Price Administration, serving until 1944, and of the Manhattan Civilian Defense, serving until 1945. In 1944 he was elected to Congress, representing New York's newly created Twenty-second (later Eighteenth) District. Powell became a member of the Seventy-ninth Congress on January 3, 1945. During his first term he served on the Indian Affairs, Invalid Pensions and Labor committees. In 1947 he took a seat on the Education and Labor Committee and sat on the Committee on Interior and Insular Affairs from 1955 to 1961.

Soon after his arrival in Washington, Powell challenged the informal regulations forbidding black representatives from using Capitol facilities reserved for members only. Following the lead of Oscar De Priest, Powell took black constituents to dine with him in the "whites only" House restaurant and ordered his staff to eat there whether they were hungry or not. On the House floor, Powell clashed almost immediately with one of the chamber's most notorious segregationists, John E. Rankin of Mississippi, and introduced legislation to outlaw lynching and the poll tax and to ban discrimination in the armed forces, housing, employment and transportation. He attached an anti-discrimination clause to so many pieces of legislation that the rider became known as the Powell Amendment. Powell attended the landmark Bandung Conference of African and Asian nations in 1955. Upon his return he urged President Eisenhower and other American policy makers to take a firm stand against colonialism and pay greater attention to the emerging Third World. The following year he broke party ranks and supported Eisenhower for reelection, charging that the Democratic platform's civil rights plank was too weak. In 1958 he survived a trial for income tax evasion, which ended in a hung jury, and a determined but unsuccessful effort by New York's Tammany Hall machine to oust him in the Democratic primary.

In 1961 Powell became chairman of the Committee on Education and Labor and began the most productive and satisfying period of his congressional career. The Committee approved over fifty measures authorizing federal programs for minimum wage increases, education and training for the deaf, school lunches, vocational training, student loans and standards for wages and work hours, as well as aid to elementary and secondary education and public libraries. This legislation comprised much of the social policy of the Kennedy and Johnson administrations. By the middle of the decade, however, Powell was under attack from both long-time enemies and committee members, who expressed dismay with his erratic management of the committee budget, numerous trips abroad at public expense, absenteeism and self-imposed exile from his district where his refusal to pay a slander judgement made him subject to arrest.

On January 9, 1967, the House Democratic Caucus stripped Powell of his committee chairmanship. Furthermore, the full House refused to seat him until completion of an investigation by the Judiciary Committee. The following month, the Committee recommended that Powell be censured, fined, and deprived of seniority, but on March 1 the House rejected these proposals and voted, 307 to 116, to exclude him from the Ninetieth Congress. Powell won a special election on April 11, 1967, to fill the vacancy caused by his exclusion, but did not take his seat. He was reelected to a twelfth term in the regular November 1968 contest, but the House voted to deny him his seniority. Powell declined to take his seat when the Ninety-first Congress convened in January 1969. In June 1969 the Supreme Court ruled that the House had acted unconstitutionally when it excluded him from the Ninetieth Congress, and Powell finally returned to his seat albeit without his twenty-two years' seniority. He unsuccessfully sought renomination in the June 1970 primary and failed to get on the ballot as an independent. Powell retired as minister at the Abyssinian Baptist Church in 1971 and died in Miami on April 4, 1972.

For further reading:

Dionisopoulos, P.A. *Rebellion, Racism, and Representation: The Adam Clayton Powell Case and Its Antecedents.* DeKalb: Northern Illinois University Press, 1970.

Lewis, Claude. *Adam Clayton Powell.* Greenwich, Conn.: Fawcett Publications, Inc., 1963.

Powell, Adam Clayton, Jr. *Adam by Adam.* New York: The Dial Press, 1971.

JOSEPH HAYNE RAINEY

United States Representative
Republican of South Carolina
Forty-first—Forty-fifth Congresses

Joseph Hayne Rainey of South Carolina was the first black to be elected to the House of Representatives and take his seat. He was born to slave parents in Georgetown, South Carolina, on June 21, 1832. Rainey's father Edward purchased his family's freedom and taught his son the barber's trade. In 1846 the Rainey family moved to Charleston. Rainey may have lived for a time in Philadelphia, and it was there that he married a woman named Susan in 1859. During the Civil War South Carolina drafted him to provision food and serve passengers on a Confederate blockade runner and to work on the fortifications of Charleston. In 1862 he and his wife escaped on a blockade runner to Bermuda, where slavery had been abolished in 1834. They settled in St. Georges, where Rainey resumed barbering. He used his acquaintance with sailors and blockade runners to keep in touch with events in South Carolina. The Raineys returned to the state in 1866 and moved to Georgetown the following year. Joseph Rainey soon became a member of the executive committee of the South Carolina Republican party and was a representative from Georgetown at the 1868 South Carolina Constitutional Convention. He was elected to a four-year term in the state senate in 1870 and was chairman of the finance committee.

After Congressman Benjamin F. Whittemore resigned in February 1870 amid charges that he had sold appointments to the United States military academies, First District Republicans nominated Rainey, who defeated Democrat C.W. Dudley in a special election and was sworn into the Forty-first Congress on December 12, 1870. He joined the Committee on Freedmen's Affairs and held his seat through the Forty-third Congress. He spoke in favor of Senator Charles Sumner's civil rights legislation that outlawed racial discrimination in juries, schools, transportation and public accommodations. Rainey insisted that unless civil rights measures were enacted he could not support amnesty bills permitting former Confederates to participate in political life. Rainey was also a warm supporter of the acts authorizing the president to call on the military to protect black voters from the threats and violence of the Ku Klux Klan.

In 1872 Rainey was reelected to the Forty-third Congress without opposition. During debate on the Indian Appropriation bill in May 1874 Rainey replaced Speaker James G. Blaine in the chair and became the first black representative to preside over a House session. A member of the Committee on Indian Affairs, he had a special interest in the subject being discussed that day.

In 1874 Rainey won a narrow reelection victory over Samuel Lee, an Independent Democrat. Lee asked the House Committee on Elections to void 669 Rainey ballots, but it held in May 1876 that Rainey had been duly elected. In the Forty-fourth Congress Rainey served on the Invalid Pensions Committee and the Select Committee on Centennial Celebration and Proposed National Census of 1875. He strongly condemned the July 4, 1876, massacre of black militiamen at Hamburg, South Carolina.

In 1876 Rainey defeated Democrat John S. Richardson, who claimed that he was entitled to the seat because of voter intimidation exercised by federal soldiers (sent to the state in response to the Hamburg massacre), by armed black political clubs and by the black militia. Richardson also claimed that his election had been certified by the governor. Rainey maintained that only the South Carolina secretary of state, who had certified his election, had the legal right to authorize the winner in a congressional race. While the case was being considered Rainey entered the Forty-fifth Congress in 1877 as a member of the Invalid Pensions Committee and the Select Committee on Enrolled Bills. He defended the use of federal troops in South Carolina during the election of 1876. He opposed an amendment to the charter of the Freedmen's Savings and Trust Company (Freedmen's Bank) that would have allowed half of its deposits to be invested in commercial paper monies. The Committee on Elections finally concluded in May 1878 that so many election irregularities had taken place in the First District that the seat should be declared vacant, but the full House referred the report back to the Committee, ensuring that Rainey would retain his seat. Rainey, however, was defeated by Richardson in 1878 as the Democratic party solidified its control in post-Reconstruction South Carolina.

After leaving his seat on March 3, 1879, Rainey received promises of Republican support for the position of Clerk of the House of Representatives, but Democratic control of the Forty-sixth Congress ruled out his appointment. Instead Rainey became an internal revenue agent in South Carolina for two years. When the Republicans regained control of the House in 1881 he spent time in Washington trying to secure his promised appointment, but his name was not placed in nomination. He remained in Washington and established a brokerage and banking firm. After the collapse of his firm, he managed a coal and wood yard before he returned to South Carolina, poor and in ill health. To provide their family with support, Susan Rainey opened a womens' hat business in Georgetown, where Joseph Rainey died on August 2, 1887.

For further reading:

Packwood, Cyril Outerbridge. *Detour—Bermuda, Destination—U.S. House of Representatives; The Life of Joseph Hayne Rainey.* Hamilton, Bermuda: Baxter's Limited, 1977.

CHARLES BERNARD RANGEL

(Office of Representative Rangel)

*United States Representative
Democrat of New York
Ninety-second—One Hundred First Congresses*

A leader in national efforts to halt the spread of drug addiction and drug-related crime, Charles Rangel was born in New York City on June 11, 1930. He attended De Witt Clinton High School and in 1948 entered the United States Army, serving with the Second Infantry Division in Korea. Following his discharge as a staff sergeant in 1952, Rangel graduated from high school in 1953, received a B.S. degree from the New York University School of Commerce in 1957 and earned a LL.D. degree from St. John's University in 1960. Rangel was admitted to the bar the same year and commenced practice in New York City. After a year as an assistant United States Attorney for the Southern District of New York he served as counsel to the speaker of the New York state assembly in 1965, and as counsel to the President's Commission to Revise the Draft Laws. In 1966 Rangel, a legal advisor to many figures in the civil rights movement, was elected to the first of two terms in the state assembly, representing the Seventy-second District.

In February 1970 Rangel entered the Democratic primary in New York's Eighteenth (now Sixteenth) Congressional District, challenging Representative Adam Clayton Powell, who had served almost continually in the House for a quarter of a century. After narrowly winning the primary Rangel was elected easily in November and began his congressional service on January 3, 1971. Concerned about the impact of drug-related crime on the nation's urban areas, Rangel opposed any action that might lead to the legalization of heroin and fought to decrease United States military and financial aid to countries that failed to take part in international efforts to control the illegal drug trade. Elected chair of the Congressional Black Caucus in 1974, Rangel also received national attention for his service on the House Judiciary Committee's hearings on the impeachment of President Nixon.

When the Ninety-eighth Congress convened in 1983, Rangel became chairman of the Select Committee on Narcotics Abuse and Control. He criticized proposed cutbacks in the government's anti-drug budget while attempting to secure increased grants to state and localities for the construction of shelters for the homeless. In 1986 the House adopted his amendment to the Omnibus Drug Bill calling for an increase in grants to state and local law enforcement agencies. A senior member of the House Committee on Ways and Means and chairman of its Subcommittee on Select Revenue Measures, he has introduced legislation to extend for five years tax credits to businesses that employ Vietnam veterans, former prisoners, welfare recipients and economically disadvantaged workers. In 1983 Speaker Thomas P. O'Neill, Jr. appointed Rangel a Deputy Whip for the House Democratic leadership.

ALONZO JACOB RANSIER

(Moorland-Spingarn Research Center, Howard University)

United States Representative
Republican of South Carolina
Forty-third Congress

Alonzo Jacob Ransier was born free in Charleston on January 3, 1834. After receiving a limited education, he became a shipping clerk in Charleston at the age of sixteen. Ransier's employer was found guilty of violating a law restricting employment of free blacks in certain professions, but the statute was not rigidly enforced and he was fined one cent and court costs.

Following the Civil War, General Daniel Sickles, military governor of the Carolinas, appointed Ransier registrar of elections. Ransier journeyed to Washington in 1868 as part of a delegation to present Congress with a petition from a Charleston meeting of the Friends of Equal Rights. He was a delegate to the 1868 state constitutional convention and in the same year was chairman of the Republican state central committee and a presidential elector for Ulysses S. Grant. From 1868 to

1870 he served in the state house of representatives. In 1870 Ransier was nominated for lieutenant governor and won the election. As lieutenant governor he earned a reputation for honesty in an otherwise corrupt administration and for fairness as presiding officer of the legislature. He urged blacks to resist efforts to enlist their support for the Liberal Republican presidential candidacy of Horace Greeley, despite the fact that Senator Charles Sumner, whom blacks greatly admired, was a leader of the insurgent movement. In August 1872 Second District Republicans chose Ransier to run for Congress. He easily defeated a former Union soldier, General William Gurney, who ran as an Independent Republican.

Ransier entered the House on March 3, 1873, and served on the Committee on Manufactures. He introduced measures to erect a public building in Beaufort, South Carolina, and to rebuild the west wing of the Citadel Academy in Charleston. Ransier also worked for passage of a bill authorizing $100,000 to improve Charleston harbor. None of Ransier's legislative initiatives were successful. He supported efforts to rescind federal pay increases, raise the tariff and to limit the presidency to a single six-year term.

Ransier participated in debate when the House took up a civil rights bill introduced in the Senate by Charles Sumner in December 1873. The bill's purpose was to supplement the Civil Rights Act of 1866 by prohibiting all forms of racial discrimination. After John T. Harris of Virginia declared that it was impossible for anyone on the House floor to state honestly that blacks were his equal, Ransier immediately responded that he could. (Harris replied that he had been speaking to the white men of the House).

On February 7, 1874, Ransier delivered before the House a speech that was later reprinted in pamphlet form. Speaking in support of Sumner's bill, he reminded his colleagues that in national conventions and in mass meetings throughout the South, black Americans had voiced their hopes that the federal government would oversee efforts to end racial discrimination. Blacks also had demonstrated their expectation of racial harmony, Ransier asserted, by resisting proposals to impose political restrictions on former slaveholders. Responding to attacks by Democratic congressmen from Georgia, North Carolina and New York, he vigorously defended the record of black soldiers who had fought for the Union during the Civil War. Ransier recalled the overwhelming black support for President Grant in his 1872 reelection bid and urged the Republican Party to reward these loyal voters by passing civil rights legislation.

Ransier was particularly concerned with the section of the civil rights bill designed to discourage segregation in public schools. The experience of schools ranging from Oberlin and Wilberforce to Harvard and Yale had proved the advantages of integrated education. Ransier was so disappointed with the final version of the bill, which omitted an education clause, that he abstained from voting.

By the time of his reelection campaign in 1874, Ransier allied himself with those who were trying to reform the South Carolina Republican party. He was particularly critical of the leadership of Governor Franklin J. Moses, Jr. Ransier's insurgency probably cost him the nomination that was won by Charles W. Buttz. Although Ransier bitterly claimed Buttz had spent four thousand dollars to win the nomination, he supported the Republican ticket in November.

Soon after leaving Congress, Ransier's wife Louisa died following the birth of their eleventh child (named after Charles Sumner). Although he managed to secure an appointment as United States internal revenue collector for the second district of South Carolina in 1875 and 1876, he later fell into poverty. He worked in Charleston as a night watchman at the Custom House and as a municipal street sweeper before his death on August 17, 1882, at age 48.

JAMES THOMAS RAPIER

(Moorland-Spingarn Research Center, Howard University)

United States Representative
Republican of Alabama
Forty-third Congress

James Thomas Rapier was born in Florence, Lauderdale County, Alabama, on November 13, 1837, the fourth child and youngest son of John H. Rapier, a barber who had been manumitted in 1829, and his wife Susan, a free black. John Rapier was able to send James and another son to a black school in Nashville for six years. After two years as a roustabout on the Mississippi, James Rapier entered school at the experimental black community of Buxton, Ontario, in 1856 and later attended a normal institute in Toronto. At Buxton he experienced a religious conversion and resolved to devote his life to aiding southern blacks. Receiving a teaching certificate in 1863, he returned to Buxton as an instructor. In late 1864 he went to Nashville and after a brief stint as a reporter for a northern newspaper became a cotton planter on 200 acres of rented land in Maury County, Tennessee.

Rapier entered politics in August 1865, giving the keynote address at the Tennessee Negro Suffrage Convention in Nashville. Unhappy with Tennessee's failure to grant blacks the franchise, Rapier returned to Alabama, where he rented 550 acres on Seven Mile Island in the Tennessee River and became a successful cotton planter. With his newfound prosperity, he offered sharecroppers low-interest loans and established a Republican newspaper in Montgomery. Soon he reentered politics, organizing recently-franchised blacks and serving as platform committee chairman at the first Alabama Republican state convention. In a plea for moderation, he opposed the total disfranchisement of whites who had helped the Confederacy and rejected the redistribution and confiscation of land. In October 1867 he was elected a delegate to Alabama's constitutional convention, where he favored full citizenship rights for blacks. Defying threats against his life, he worked for the national Republican ticket in 1868, but was falsely accused in September of conspiring to burn the Tuscumbia Female Academy. Rapier was forced to flee Lauderdale County for Montgomery, where he remained in obscurity for a year. Cleared of all charges, he traveled to Washington in 1869 to attend the founding convention of the National Negro Labor Union (N.N.L.U.), an organization formed to protect black laborers, help sharecroppers acquire land, and improve educational and economic opportunities for blacks.

In 1870, Rapier became the Republican candidate for secretary of state and was the first black to run for state-wide office in Alabama. Defeated after a hard-fought campaign, he accepted a federal appointment as an internal revenue assessor and helped organize the Alabama Negro Labor Union, a group associated with the N.N.L.U. In August 1872, Republicans of the Second Congressional District in southeast and south central Alabama nominated him for Congress. In November he defeated Democrat William C. Oates to become Alabama's second black representative. With a year to wait until the Forty-third Congress convened, Rapier journeyed to Vienna in May 1873 as Alabama's commissioner to the Fifth International Exposition. He returned in September and was present on December 1 to take his seat in the House and to accept assignment as a member of the Committee on Education and Labor.

Perhaps Rapier's greatest legislative achievement was securing passage of the Montgomery Port Bill that designated the Alabama capital a port of delivery managed by a federally appointed collector of customs. On other economic issues, he sided with fellow southerners in favoring railroad regulation, opposing tight money and calling for an increase in currency circulation. He sponsored unsuccessful legislation to set up a federal fund to help southern common schools fight illiteracy and educate blacks. Rapier joined Education and Labor Committee colleagues in calling on Congress to ensure proper financial management at Auburn Agricultural and Mechanical College in his state and at other southern land grant colleges. He worked for passage of a new Civil Rights Act, holding strategy meetings at his lodgings and taking to the House floor to describe the discrimination and physical threats that he had experienced on his way from Montgomery to Washington.

Rapier returned to Alabama in July and, although hampered by divisions among Second District Republicans, immediately entered into what promised to be a tough campaign for reelection. His pleas to federal authorities for help in ensuring a peaceful election fell on deaf ears. The poll itself was marred by the incidents of stolen and destroyed ballot boxes, bribery, fraudulent counts, armed intimidation and murder that all too often characterized elections in the Reconstruction South. An attorney and former Confederate army major, Jeremiah Williams, edged Rapier in the balloting. The defeated incumbent contested the result without success. After the lame duck session of Congress began in December, it passed the civil rights bill Rapier and others had worked so hard for, albeit in a watered down version.

In 1876 Rapier moved to Lowndes County near Montgomery and ran again for the House from the Fourth District, which remained the only black majority district in

Alabama as a result of a redistricting plan enacted by the Democratic legislature. Rapier won the Republican nomination over the incumbent representative, Jeremiah Haralson, who then ran as an independent, splitting the district's black vote and ensuring the election of Democrat Charles Shelley. Rapier never stood for public office again.

In July 1878 Rapier's loyalty to the Republican Party was rewarded with his appointment as Collector of Internal Revenue for the Second District. By this time Rapier had become an ardent advocate of black emigration to the West. At the Southern States Negro Convention in May 1879, he chaired the migration committee and exhorted blacks to join the "Exodusters," as they were called, in leaving the South for the Great Plains. He lent the movement tangible support, using the profits from his cotton lands to bankroll parties of emigrants, inspecting land in Kansas for blacks to settle on and analyzing the situation for the Senate Emigration Committee. Faced with increasingly poor health, Rapier remained in Alabama and campaigned for state and national Republican candidates while resisting the efforts of white conservatives to attain control of Alabama's Republican Party.

During 1882 and 1883 Rapier managed to fight off an attempt by his enemies to remove him from the Collector's post, but his worsening physical condition soon forced him to resign. He was appointed disbursing officer for a Montgomery government building shortly before his death from tuberculosis on May 31, 1883, at age 46.

For further reading:

Schweninger, Loren. *James T. Rapier and Reconstruction.* Chicago: The University of Chicago Press, 1978.

HIRAM RHODES REVELS

(U.S. Senate Historical Office)

United States Senator
Republican of Mississippi
Forty-first Congress

Hiram Revels, the first black member of the United States Senate, was born in Fayetteville, North Carolina, of free parents, on September 27, 1827. Revels attended various schools and seminaries and Knox College in Galesburg, Illinois. He was ordained a minister in the African Methodist Episcopal Church at Baltimore in 1845 and carried on religious work in Indiana, Illinois, Kansas, Kentucky, Tennessee, and Maryland before accepting a pastorate in Baltimore in 1860. At the outbreak of the Civil War he assisted in recruiting two black regiments in Maryland. Revels served in Vicksburg, Mississippi, as chaplain of a black regiment and organized black churches in Mississippi. In 1863 he established a school for freedmen in St. Louis. After serving churches in Louisville and New Orleans, Revels settled in Natchez in 1866 and was elected an alderman in 1868. In 1869 he was elected to represent Adams County in the state senate.

On January 20, 1870, Revels was chosen by a legislative vote of eighty-five to fifteen to fill the unexpired term of former Confederate president Jefferson Davis in the United States Senate. Revels' opponents in the Senate struggled to block his seating. Some contended that he had not become a full-fledged citizen until passage of the Fourteenth Amendment in 1866 and thus failed to meet the nine years' citizenship requirement of Article One, Section Three of the Constitution. Others claimed that his election was null and void, inasmuch as Mississippi was without civil government because of military rule. Still others asserted that his credentials were invalid because they had been signed by an unelected military governor. A majority of senators rejected these arguments, and on February 25 Revels was seated by a vote of forty-eight to eight.

During his brief Senate term Revels was a member of the Committee on Education and Labor and the Committee on the District of Columbia. He generally believed that Christian education, high morals and abstinence from alcohol, rather than agitation for political and civil rights, were the best ways for blacks to improve their condition. His maiden speech was a plea for the reinstatement of black legislators who had been prevented from serving in the Georgia General Assembly. Revels favored amnesty and the restoration of full citizenship rights to ex-Confederates who swore loyalty to the United States. He nominated a black candidate from Mississippi, Michael Howard, to the United States Military Academy, but Howard was not admitted. He introduced legislation to increase cotton production by appropriating $2 million and five million acres of public land for levee repair on the Mississippi. When Senator Allen G. Thurman of Ohio submitted an amendment that would have perpetuated the segregation of Washington, D.C.'s public schools, Revels spoke against it, maintaining that integrated education would not lead to social equality between blacks and whites. He came to the aid of black mechanics who were barred from work at the Washington Navy Yard because of their color and also submitted a number of private petitions for removal of political disabilities and for relief of war claims.

A year after Revels' term expired on March 3, 1871, he became the first president of Alcorn University, the first land-grant college in the United States for black students. He left Alcorn briefly to serve as Mississippi's secretary of state ad interim during 1873. The following year he resigned from Alcorn to avoid dismissal by Republican governor Adelbert Ames, a political enemy, and became pastor of a church in Holly Springs. His racial conservatism, his anger at Ames and dismay with the corruption of some Republicans as well as hopes of regaining the presidency of Alcorn, led Revels to campaign for several Democrats during the state election of 1875. When the Senate's Select Committee to Inquire into Alleged Frauds in Recent Elections in Mississippi questioned him the following year, Revels falsely testified that conditions had been relatively peaceful and that he was unaware of any widespread violence. Both of these stances were political blunders that cost Revels his pastorate at Holly Springs and the respect and support of many black Mississippians. With the aid of Democratic governor John M. Stone, Revels returned to Alcorn in July 1876. He retired in 1882 and returned to his former church at Holly Springs while teaching theology at Shaw (later Rust) University and continuing his religious work as an A.M.E. district superintendent. He died in Aberdeen, Mississippi, on January 16, 1901.

For further reading:

Libby, Billy W. "Senator Hiram R. Revels of Mississippi Takes His Seat, January-February, 1870." *Journal of Mississippi History* 37 (November 1975): pp. 381–394.

Singer, Donald L. "For Whites Only: The Seating of Hiram Revels in the United States Senate." *Negro History Bulletin* 35 (March 1972): pp. 61–63.

Thompson, Julius Eric. *Hiram R. Revels, 1827–1901: A Biography.* Ph.D. dissertation, Princeton University, 1973. Reprint. New York: Arno Press, 1982.

GUS SAVAGE

(Office of Representative Savage)

United States Representative

Democrat of Illinois

Ninety-seventh—One Hundred First Congresses

Gus Savage's election to Congress in 1980 was another milepost in a long career as a pioneer black journalist and community and civil rights leader. Born in Detroit on October 30, 1925, Savage attended the public schools of Chicago and graduated from Wendell Phillips High School in 1943. He served in the United States Army from 1943 to 1946 before earning a B.A. degree in philosophy from Roosevelt University in 1951. He attended Chicago-Kent College of Law during 1952–1953 and began his career as a journalist in 1954.

Savage entered political life in the late 1940s as a fulltime organizer for the Progressive Party of former Vice President Henry A. Wallace. He also promoted programs for Paul Robeson, Dr. Martin Luther King, and Hon. Elijah Muhammad. He was a lifelong civil rights advocate and fought against discrimination in housing, hiring and in labor unions, serving in the 1960s as chairman of Chicago's South End Voters Conference, campaign manager for the Midwest League of Negro Voters and as chairman of Protest at the Polls. Beginning in 1965, Savage owned and edited Citizen Newspapers, a chain of independent community weeklies. As the only black journalist currently serving in Congress, he continues to write a regular column which appears in approximately 150 black newspapers. He also broadcasts a weekly radio commentary.

A determined foe of Chicago's Democratic machine, Savage ran for Congress in Illinois' Third Congressional District in 1968 but lost the primary to incumbent Representative William T. Murphy. A 1970 primary bid was also unsuccessful. After Second District Representative Morgan F. Murphy announced his retirement in December 1979, Savage entered the race to succeed him, defeating a machine-backed candidate and two other opponents in the primary and winning the general election with eighty-eight percent of the vote.

Savage became a member of Congress on January 3, 1981, and is chairman of the Committee on Public Works and Transportation Subcommittee on Economic Development. He is also the senior black member of the Committee on Small Business. In 1986 he successfully sponsored an amendment to the National Defense Authorization Act for Fiscal Year 1987, which imposed the largest federal contract set-aside program in history on all military procurement, providing a possible $25 billion for minority-owned and controlled businesses, institutions, and historically black colleges.

ROBERT SMALLS

United States Representative
Republican of South Carolina
Forty-fourth—Forty-fifth, Forty-seventh—Forty-ninth Congresses

Robert Smalls was born a slave on April 5, 1839, in Beaufort, a coastal town in the Sea Islands of South Carolina. He moved to Charleston in 1851 and worked on the waterfront as a stevedore, foreman, sailmaker, rigger and sailor before becoming an expert pilot of boats along the coasts of South Carolina and Georgia. When the Civil War began he was impressed into service on the cotton steamer *Planter*. On May 13, 1862, he and his black crew slipped the *Planter* past Confederate guns and turned it over to the Union fleet, an act that won him national fame.

Smalls' heroic wartime record, his ability to speak the Gullah dialect of Sea Islanders, and the solidly Republican electorate around Beaufort opened the way for a post-war career in politics. As early as October 1862 Smalls traveled to New York to gain support for the Port Royal Experiment for settling freed slaves, and he joined a delegation of free blacks sent to the Republican convention in June 1864. Following the Civil War, he was elected a delegate to the 1868 state constitutional convention and in April 1868 was elected to the state house of representatives, serving until 1870. He subsequently was a member of the state senate from 1870 to 1874. His political career culminated in 1874 with election to Congress from the Fifth District over Independent candidate J.P.M. Epping.

Smalls took his seat in the Forty-fourth Congress on March 4, 1875, and served on the Agriculture Committee. He succeeded in having the harbor at Port Royal, South Carolina, designated as the southern rendezvous for the United States Navy. He fought against the transfer of federal troops from the South to the Texas frontier, warning that their removal would encourage private militia groups to take the law into their own hands and declare open warfare on citizens loyal to the Reconstruction governments. He also opposed racial discrimination in the armed services.

Smalls won reelection in 1876 over Democrat George D. Tillman. During the campaign he resisted Democratic attempts to "redeem" South Carolina by driving blacks from public life. Smalls managed to retain his seat despite efforts by Tillman to have the House overturn the results. During the last session of the Forty-fourth Congress in February 1877, Smalls delivered a major address calling for an "honest ballot," praising the Republican state government of South Carolina and decrying efforts to deprive blacks of their political and economic rights. After regaining control of the state, Democrats seeking Smalls' resignation from Congress gained his conviction on false charges of having received a $5,000 bribe while in the state senate. Smalls was jailed briefly but pardoned by Democratic governor William D. Simpson, who acted on assurances from the United States district attorney that South Carolinians accused of violating election laws would not be prosecuted.

The abolition of voting precincts in counties with a Republican majority and the presence of armed whites who harassed the largely black audiences at his election meetings doomed Smalls' bid for reelection in 1878. Although he was beaten by Tillman, he stood for election to the seat again in 1880. Narrowly defeated, he successfully contested the result and was finally seated in the Forty-seventh Congress on July 19, 1882, and served on the Committee on Agriculture and the Committee on the Militia.

In September Smalls was defeated for the Republican nomination at the Seventh District convention by Edmund W.M. Mackey. When Mackey died in January 1884 Smalls was elected to fill the vacancy and took his seat in the Forty-eighth Congress on March 18, 1884. He was a member of the Committees on Manufactures and on the Militia. Later that year he won reelection to a full term over William Elliott and in December was nominated for the United States Senate by black legislators. He lost the Senate nomination to Wade Hampton by a vote of 31 to 3. In the Forty-ninth Congress he served on the Committee on War Claims and tried to secure for South Carolina a full refund of money collected from the state during the war years. He supported an amendment to interstate commerce legislation sponsored by Representative James E. O'Hara of North Carolina, requiring equal accommodations for all railroad passengers regardless of their color, and sought legislation guaranteeing integration of eating places in the District of Columbia. Smalls asked the House to defy President Cleveland and approve a fifty dollar monthly pension for the widow of General David Hunter, who in 1862 had issued an order freeing slaves in Florida, Georgia and South Carolina and had authorized the raising of one of the earliest black regiments, the First South Carolina. Smalls also reaffirmed his party loyalty by opposing Democratic-sponsored proposals for civil service reform.

By 1886 President Cleveland, Governor John P. Richardson, Senator Wade Hampton, and First District Congressman Samuel Dibble determined to unseat Smalls. Aided by their efforts and weakening in Republican solidarity, Elliott won the election. Once more Smalls took his case to the House, which declined to unseat Elliott. Smalls remained politically active and joined other black leaders in their vain fight against disfranchisement at the state constitutional convention of 1895. He also advised South Carolina blacks against joining the "Exodusters" emigrating to Kansas. In 1889 President Harrison appointed Smalls collector of the port of Beaufort. He held this post almost continuously until the opposition of South Carolina senators Benjamin Tillman (brother of George D. Tillman) and Ellison D. Smith forced him to step down in June 1913. He died in Beaufort on February 22, 1915.

For further reading:

Uya, Okon Edet. *From Slavery To Public Service: Robert Smalls, 1839-1915*. New York: Oxford University Press, 1971.

BENNETT McVEY STEWART

United States Representative
Democrat of Illinois
Ninety-sixth Congress

Bennett McVey Stewart was born in Huntsville, Alabama, on August 6, 1912. He attended public schools in Huntsville, graduated from high school in Birmingham and received a B.A. from Miles College in 1936. From 1936 to 1938 he served as assistant principal of Irondale High School in Birmingham. Stewart returned to Miles College as an associate professor of sociology from 1938 until 1940, when he joined an insurance company as an executive. In 1950 he became Illinois state director for the company, a position he held for eighteen years. He retired from the insurance business to become an inspector with the city of Chicago's building department and a rehabilitation specialist with the Chicago department of urban renewal, advising property owners on the financing of renovations. This position soon led to involvement with politics. He was elected to the Chicago City Council as an alderman from the Twenty-first Ward in 1971 and was elected Democratic committeeman for the same ward in 1972, holding both offices until 1978.

After Representative Ralph H. Metcalfe, Sr., died in October 1978, Stewart was chosen by the ten Democratic ward committeemen from the First Congressional District as the party's candidate to fill the vacancy. He defeated former alderman A.A. Rayner in the November election and became a member of the Ninety-sixth Congress on January 3, 1979, serving on the Committee on Appropriations. He supported federal loan guarantees to the financially troubled Chrysler Corporation, which employed more than 1,500 workers in the First District. Stewart evidenced his concern for low-income citizens by advocating emergency appropriations to provide low-income people with home heating assistance and by trying to extend the time participants could spend in public service employment programs.

Following allegations of mismanagement in the Chicago Housing Authority, Stewart sought and received a General Accounting Office analysis of the city agency. The 1980 study revealed that management had been so unsatisfactory that the Authority had been driven to the verge of bankruptcy. He carried on the efforts of Ralph Metcalfe and reintroduced his resolution designating February as Black History Month. Stewart also spoke out against a proposed constitutional amendment to prohibit public school busing. Recalling the humiliations of segregation he had experienced growing up in Birmingham, he attacked the proposal as a subversion of the Fourteenth Amendment and an attempt to reestablish segregation in the United States.

Stewart attempted to win a second term but was defeated in the March 1980 primary by Harold Washington. After leaving Congress he served as interim director of the Chicago Department of Inter-Governmental Affairs from 1981 to 1983 before retiring from public life. He remained a resident of Chicago until his death there on April 26, 1988.

LOUIS STOKES

(Office of Representative Stokes)

United States Representative
Democrat of Ohio
Ninety-first—One Hundred First Congresses

The first black representative from Ohio and the current dean of Ohio's Democratic congressional delegation, Louis Stokes was born in Cleveland on February 23, 1925. He attended Cleveland's public schools and served in the United States Army from 1943 to 1946 before attending Western Reserve University from 1946 to 1948. After receiving a Doctor of Law degree from Cleveland Marshall Law School of the Cleveland State University in 1953, Stokes was admitted to the bar the same year and commenced practice in Cleveland. Stokes was active in the 1960s civil rights movement, serving as vice president of the Cleveland branch of the National Association for the Advancement of Colored People during 1965–1966, and as chairman of its Legal Redress Committee for five years.

Following a suit argued by Stokes on behalf of Republican leader Charles P. Lucas, the United States Supreme Court ruled in December 1967 requiring the Ohio legislature to adopt a congressional redistricting plan that accurately reflected the presence of black voters. A new district, the Twenty-first, was subsequently created, and Stokes won the Democratic nomination over a field of twenty opponents in the May 1968 primary. He defeated Lucas in the general election. Sworn into Congress on January 3, 1969, Stokes served on the Education and Labor Committee and on the House Un-American Activities Committee (renamed the House Internal Security Committee in 1969). In 1971 Stokes was elected to the Appropriations Committee, becoming the first black member of Congress to join the panel. When the House Budget Committee was formed in 1974, Stokes was among those elected to membership. In 1972 he became chairman of the Congressional Black Caucus and served two consecutive terms.

During his ten terms in Congress, Stokes has headed and participated in several major House investigations. In March 1977 he was appointed to lead the Select Committee on Assassinations, formed to conduct an investigation of the circumstances surrounding the deaths of President John F. Kennedy and Dr. Martin Luther King, Jr. The committee concluded its work in December 1978 with twenty-seven volumes of hearings and a final report containing recommendations for administrative and legislative reform. During the Ninety-seventh and Ninety-eighth Congresses (1981–1985), Stokes was chairman of the House Committee on Standards of Official Conduct (Ethics Committee). In 1983, when the United States invaded Grenada, Stokes was chosen as a member of the House panel to visit the island and investigate the military operation. He was appointed chairman of the House Permanent Select Committee on Intelligence in January 1987, and in the same month became a member of the House Select Committee to Investigate Covert Arms Transactions with Iran.

EDOLPHUS TOWNS

(Office of Representative Towns)

United States Representative

Democrat of New York

Ninety-eighth—One Hundred First Congresses

A long-time civic leader and former borough president of Brooklyn, Edolphus "Ed" Towns entered Congress in January 1983. Towns was born in Chadbourn, North Carolina, on July 21, 1934. After attending Chadbourn's public schools he earned a B.S. degree from North Carolina A.&T. in 1956. Following two years of service in the United States Army, Towns taught in New York City's public schools and at Fordham University and Medgar Evers College of the City University of New York. He was a program director at Metropolitan Hospital and served as the assistant administrator at Beth Israel Hospital from 1965 through 1975. Towns also worked in Brooklyn with educational and health care groups and with programs for youth and senior citizens.

Towns' varied civic activities helped lead to his election in 1972 as the Democratic state committeeman for the Fortieth Assembly District, a position he held until his election to Congress. In 1973 he received a master's degree in social work from Adelphi University. From 1976 to 1982 Towns served as the first black deputy borough president of Brooklyn. When Representative Frederick W. Richmond resigned from the House in August 1982, Towns entered the race to succeed him and was elected to represent the Eleventh Congressional District in November. During his tenure in Congress, Towns has served as both treasurer and vice chairman of the Congressional Black Caucus. He has been responsible for the enactment of legislation related to bilingual education, limited resource farmers, 1890 land grant institutions, and animal rights. He is currently a member of the Committee on Government Operations, the Committee on Public Works and Transportation, and the Select Committee on Narcotics Abuse and Control.

BENJAMIN STERLING TURNER

(Library of Congress)

United States Representative
Republican of Alabama
Forty-second Congress

Benjamin Sterling Turner was the first black member of the House of Representatives from Alabama. He was born a slave in Weldon, Halifax County, North Carolina, on March 17, 1825, and was taken to Alabama at the age of five. There he surreptitiously managed to secure an education. He eventually settled in Selma, where he became a merchant and owned a livery stable. In 1867 he was elected tax collector of Dallas County and by 1869 was a Selma city councilman. The next year he won election as a Republican Representative from Alabama's First Congressional District.

During the Forty-second Congress, Turner introduced a bill that would have removed legal and political disabilities imposed on former Confederates by Section Three of the Fourteenth Amendment, but the House never considered his proposal. He also sponsored legislation to appropriate $200,000 for construction of a federal building in Selma and a bill for relief of St. Paul's Episcopal Church in the same city. Turner's membership on the Committee on Invalid Pensions helped him secure passage by the full House of two private pension bills, one of which put a corporal of a Civil War black regiment on the pension roll at eight dollars a month.

On February 20, 1872, Turner presented to the House a petition from the Mobile board of trade asking for a refund of the cotton tax collected from Southern states from 1866 to 1868. On May 31 he addressed the House on this subject, attacking the tax as unconstitutional and decrying its harmful effect on the already meager income of cotton field workers, the vast majority of whom, he pointed out, were southern blacks. The same day he called on the federal government to buy large private land tracts at public auction and then to subdivide the land into tracts of not more than 160 acres to be sold to landless southern freedmen. No action was taken on either of these proposals.

In 1872 Turner won renomination, but another black candidate, Philip Joseph, launched an independent campaign for the seat. Frederick G. Bromberg, candidate of the Democrats and Liberal Republicans, benefited from a divided black vote and won the seat.

Turner returned to Alabama, took up farming, and confined his political activities to the county level, reemerging only briefly as a delegate to the 1880 Republican National Convention in Chicago. He died in Selma on March 21, 1894.

ALTON RONALD WALDON, Jr.

(Congressional Black Caucus)

United States Representative
Democrat of New York
Ninety-ninth Congress

Alton Waldon was born on December 21, 1936, in Lakeland, Florida. He joined the United States Army in 1956 and was discharged as a Specialist 4 in 1959. Waldon received a B.S. from John Jay College in 1968 and a J.D. from New York Law School in 1973. He joined the New York City Housing Authority's police force in 1962 and served until 1975, when he was appointed deputy commissioner of the State Division of Human Rights. During 1981 and 1982 he also served as assistant counsel for the Office of Mental Retardation and Developmental Disabilities. In 1982 he was elected to represent the Thirty-third District in the New York assembly, where he served until his election to Congress.

In May 1986 Waldon was nominated by Queens Democratic leaders in the Sixth Congressional District to run for the seat left vacant by the death of Representative Joseph Addabbo. In a close special election decided by absentee ballots, Waldon was declared the victor over Floyd H. Flake and was sworn in as a member of the Ninety-ninth Congress on July 29, 1986. He took seats on the Committee on Education and Labor and Committee on Small Business. He called on the House to override the presidential veto of legislative sanctions against the government of South Africa and opposed covert aid to Angolan rebels who were supported by South Africa's white minority regime. Waldon also introduced a resolution calling on President Reagan to participate in a summit with leaders of countries bordering South Africa. He supported proposals for combating drug abuse, with particular emphasis on the menace of the cocaine compound "crack," and sponsored a resolution that urged the formation of a national task force on the problem of functional illiteracy.

Waldon stood for renomination in the September 1986 Democratic primary but lost to Flake, who went on to win the seat in the general election. Following the end of his term he was appointed to the New York State Investigation Commission.

JOSIAH THOMAS WALLS

(Library of Congress)

*United States Representative
Republican of Florida
Forty-second, Forty-third—Forty-fourth Congresses*

The only black representative from Florida, Josiah Thomas Walls had the unfortunate distinction of being the only black congressman to be unseated twice by opponents who contested his election. He was born, probably in slavery, in or near Winchester, Virginia, on December 30, 1842. As a child, Walls moved to Darkesville in what is now West Virginia. Walls briefly attended the county normal school in Harrisburg, Pennsylvania, and may have received additional education. As a congressman, Walls described his impressment into the Confederate army and his capture by Northern forces at the siege of Yorktown, Virginia, in May 1862. By July 1863 he had entered the Third Infantry Regiment, United States Colored Troops at Philadelphia, becoming a corporal in October. Walls moved with his regiment to Florida in February 1864. After his discharge in October 1865 he worked at a sawmill on the Suwannee river and later taught at Archer in Alachua County.

In 1867 Walls was elected to represent Alachua County at the 1868 Florida Constitutional Convention. The county convention of March 1868 also nominated Walls for the state assembly and he was elected, taking his seat in June. Later that same year he was elected to the state senate from the Thirteenth District and took his seat the following January. Walls participated in several national conventions held to discuss problems facing blacks. At the Southern States Convention of Colored Men in 1871 he proposed an amendment to a resolution of support for President Ulysses S. Grant which called on the Republicans to nominate John Mercer Langston for vice president in 1872.

In August 1870 Florida Republicans nominated Walls for the state's lone seat in the House of Representatives. Walls appeared to win a narrow election victory and presented his credentials to the Congress on March 4, 1871. He accepted assignments to the Committee on Militia, the Committee on Mileage, and the Committee on Expenditures in the Navy Department. Walls' opponent, Silas L. Niblack, disputed the election, charging that officials had unfairly rejected some of his votes while accepting Walls' illegal ballots. Walls maintained that the vote count had been fraudulent and that voters had been intimidated and physically threatened at the polls. Although the House Committee on Elections unseated Walls by declaring Niblack the winner on January 29, 1873, he held office for less than two months. Walls had already defeated him in the November 1872 election for one of Florida's two congressional seats.

Although Walls' efforts to defend his election occupied much of his time, he was still able to put forth several proposals and speak on a variety of subjects. Since he feared public education would receive little attention if it were administered by southern states, he supported a measure to establish a national educational fund financed with money from public land sales. He introduced bills for the relief of private pensioners and Seminole War veterans. He strongly favored expenditures for internal improvements in Florida and supported efforts to grant belligerent status to rebels fighting in Cuba for independence from Spain, which still permitted slavery to exist on the island.

In 1874 Walls stood for reelection against Jesse J. Finley, edging him by only 371 votes. Finley contested the election. A majority of six Democrats and one Independent Republican of the Committee on Elections reported that Walls' votes in one Columbia County precinct had been tampered with by the Republican state senate candidate—who had been mysteriously murdered in August 1875—and should be deleted from Walls' total, thereby making Finley the winner. The committee's three Republicans maintained that the disputed ballots, which had been burned in a suspicious courthouse fire, were not cast illegally and that Walls was entitled to his seat. The Democratic-controlled House adopted the majority report, and Walls' congressional career ended.

In August 1876 Walls was defeated by Horatio Bisbee for renomination to the House. In November he was elected to the state senate, where he became a champion of mandatory public education. Frustrated by his political isolation and overwhelmed with feelings of futility, Walls took an indefinite leave of absence in February 1879 and left the state senate for good.

Upon his return to Alachua County, Walls owned and operated a successful tomato and lettuce farm, sawmill and orange groves. He also remained interested in political developments. In 1884, after again being beaten by Bisbee for the Republican nomination to the House, he ran as an independent candidate but was unsuccessful. In the fall of 1890 he was defeated in another bid for the state senate. He slipped into ill health and lost his fortune when a February 1895 freeze ruined his crops. Shortly thereafter he was placed in charge of the farm at Florida Normal College (now Florida A&M University). He died in Tallahassee on May 15, 1905.

For further reading:

Klingman, Peter D. *Josiah Walls: Florida's Black Congressman of Reconstruction.* Gainesville: The University Presses of Florida, 1976.

CRAIG ANTHONY WASHINGTON

(Office of Representative Washington)

United States Representative
Democrat of Texas
One Hundred First Congress

Following the death of Mickey Leland in August 1989, Craig Washington emerged as the leading candidate to fill the seat of his long-time friend and political ally in Houston's Eighteenth District. Washington entered the non-partisan primary after Leland's widow, Alison, declined to run for the seat. The leading vote-getter in the primary, Washington easily won in the special election of December 9, 1989. He took the oath of office on January 23, 1990, at the opening of the second session of the One Hundred First Congress.

Washington was born in Longview, Texas, on October 12, 1941. He attended Prairie View A & M University in Texas and received his B.A. in 1966. In 1969 he graduated from the Thurgood Marshall School of Law at Texas Southern University. He commenced practice

153

as a criminal defense lawyer and is a partner in a Houston law firm.

Soon after embarking on his private career, Washington entered politics as a member of the Texas House of Representatives. He and Leland served together as freshmen members of the Texas legislature in 1973. Washington continued to serve in the Texas House of Representatives until election to the state Senate in 1983. As a member of the state legislature, he served as chairman of the House committees on criminal jurisprudence, social services and human services and as chairman of the Legislative Black Caucus.

In the Texas House of Representatives and the Texas Senate, Washington emerged as a commanding speaker as well as an effective legislative strategist. He was a leader on various civil rights issues, particularly the efforts to increase the participation of women and minorities in the state government. He gained passage of legislation restricting state investments in businesses dealing with South Africa and extending state poverty programs. Washington also helped coordinate the state's fight against AIDS.

Washington based his campaign for the House on the theme of "Pass the Torch" and promised to pursue the political issues associated with Mickey Leland. As a representative from the Eighteenth District, he follows in the footsteps of Barbara Jordan as well as Leland.

HAROLD WASHINGTON

(Moorland-Spingarn Research Center, Howard University)

United States Representative
Democrat of Illinois
Ninety-seventh—Ninety-eighth Congresses

Although he is chiefly remembered for being the first black to be elected mayor of Chicago, Harold Washington also served in the House of Representatives following a career as an attorney and state legislator. He was born in Chicago on April 15, 1922, attending Forrestville School and DuSable High School before his service with the United States Air Force Engineers in the Pacific from 1942 to 1946. In 1949 he received a B.A. from Roosevelt University and earned a J.D. from Northwestern University's school of law in 1952. In 1954 he succeeded his late father as a precinct captain in the Third Ward regular Democratic organization. Washington was admitted to the Illinois bar in 1953 and commenced the practice of law in Chicago, joining the city corporation counsel's office as an assistant prosecutor from 1954 to 1958. Beginning in 1960 he served for four years as an arbitrator for the Illinois State Industrial Commission. In 1965 he entered the state house of representatives, serving until his election to the state senate in 1976. In a special primary held in 1977 after the death of Richard J. Daley, Washington finished third in a field of four contenders for the Democratic nomination for mayor of Chicago.

Washington defeated incumbent Representative Bennett Stewart in the March 1980 primary and was unopposed in the general election for the House seat. On January 3, 1981, he became a member of the Ninety-seventh Congress and served on the Committee on Education and Labor, the Committee on Government Operations, and the Judiciary Committee. During the 1981 budget reconciliation process, Washington voted "present" rather than agree to an Education and Labor Committee proposal to cut $11.7 billion from student aid, employment training and child nutrition programs. On the Judiciary Committee he helped negotiate an agreement to extend enforcement sections of the 1965 Voting Rights Act which guaranteed that jurisdictions with a history of voting rights abuses would be unable to take advantage of the measure's "bail-out" provisions and escape coverage under the Act. He also voted against authorization of a refugee assistance program that did not categorize as refugees Haitians who had been detained after entering the United States illegally.

Washington began his second mayoral campaign in November 1982, shortly after his reelection to the House, and won the Democratic nomination in the February 1983 primary. Following a stormy contest that attracted national attention, Washington was elected mayor on April 12, 1983. Three weeks later he resigned from his House seat to take up his mayoral duties. He died on November 25, 1987, seven months after winning election to a second term.

For further reading:

Levinsohn, Florence Hamlish. *Harold Washington: A Political Biography.* Chicago: Chicago Review Press, 1983.

ALAN DUPREE WHEAT

United States Representative
Democrat of Missouri
Ninety-eighth—One Hundred First Congresses

In 1982 Alan Wheat became only the third freshman representative in history to be appointed to the House Committee on Rules. Wheat was born in San Antonio, Texas, on October 16, 1951. He attended schools in Wichita, Kansas, and in Seville, Spain, before graduating from Airline High School in Bossier City, Louisiana, in 1968. After receiving a B.A. in economics from Grinnell College in 1972, Wheat joined the Department of Housing and Urban Development as an economist during 1972 and 1973, and worked in the same capacity for the Mid-America Regional Council in Kansas City from 1973 to 1975. He served as an aide to Jackson County, Missouri, executive Mike White in 1975 and 1976 and was elected to the Missouri general assembly in 1976, serving three terms and chairing the urban affairs committee.

When Fifth Congressional District Representative Richard W. Bolling announced his retirement in August 1981, Wheat entered the race to succeed him and was elected to the Ninety-eighth Congress in November 1982. In addition to the Rules Committee, on which he continues to serve, Wheat is also a member of the District of Columbia Committee, and chairs the Subcommittee on Judiciary and Education. Wheat serves on the Select Committee on Children, Youth and Families and is vice chairman of the Congressional Black Caucus.

GEORGE HENRY WHITE

(Library of Congress)

United States Representative
Republican of North Carolina
Fifty-fifth—Fifty-sixth Congresses

The last former slave to serve in Congress, George Henry White's term in the House closed out the years of service for the first generation of black representatives. He was born in Rosindale, North Carolina, on December 18, 1852. Following his emancipation at age ten, White helped his family with farming and cask-making and intermittently attended public schools in Columbus County, North Carolina. In 1873 he entered the study of medicine at Howard University but soon transferred to the study of law in North Carolina. After graduation in 1877 he continued to teach and was admitted to the North Carolina bar in 1879. The following year Eighth district voters sent White to the state house of representatives, where he secured passage of legislation authorizing establishment of four normal schools for the training of black teachers. White himself became principal of the school at New Bern. In 1884 he was elected to the state senate, where he continued his efforts to improve public education. White established a second residence in Tarboro in 1886 when he was elected solicitor and prosecuting attorney for the second judicial district of North Carolina.

In 1894 White sought the Republican nomination for Congress from the Second District but lost to former representative Henry P. Cheatham, his brother-in-law. Two years later White defeated Cheatham for the nomination and was elected over Democratic congressman Frederick A. Woodard and Populist candidate, D.S. Moss.

The sole black representative to take the oath of office when the Fifty-fifth Congress met on March 15, 1897, White was a member of the Committee on Agriculture. He was aware of his unique position and spoke out on issues affecting the nation's blacks. White was particularly interested in halting the lynchings that reached record numbers in the 1890s. On January 20, 1900, he introduced an unprecedented bill to make lynching a federal crime, with both principals and accessories to a lynching liable for punishment by death. White compared lynching to treason in its gravity and cited statistics showing that blacks were far more likely to be lynched than non-blacks. Although White's bill expired in the Judiciary Committee, it marked the first step of a long struggle in Congress to enact federal anti-lynching legislation.

During his two terms in the House White sought in vain to secure financial relief for Civil War hero and former Congressman Robert Smalls and former Louisiana Governor P.B.S. Pinchback. After a large group of white men murdered the black postmaster of Lake City, South Carolina, and his baby son in February 1898, White presented a resolution for the relief of the victim's wife and five surviving children, all of whom had been wounded. Representative Charles Bartlett of Georgia objected to White's request and no action was taken. Since the state government of North Carolina had little interest in increasing awareness of black achievement, White hoped to persuade the federal government to perform the task. In December 1899 he asked that $15,000 be appropriated to defray the costs of an exhibit on black education at the 1900 Paris Exposition, but his proposal was not approved. White also directed the attention of the House to the second section of the Fourteenth Amendment and called for its use to reduce the congressional representation of states where blacks were disfranchised.

White won reelection in 1898 over Democratic and Populist opponents, but the scurrility of the congressional campaign and widespread efforts to drive blacks from public life in North Carolina persuaded him that election to a third term was impossible. He was particularly critical of the *Raleigh News and Observer*'s vicious editorial attacks and the intimidation activities of armed white supremacy groups. In his celebrated "valedictory" speech of January 29, 1901, White noted that his departure would leave Congress without any black representatives, but he predicted that one day black lawmakers would return to the Capitol.

After leaving Congress White moved from North Carolina and embarked on a remarkable second career. In addition to opening a law practice in Washington, White developed a town for blacks on 1,700 acres that he and five others had purchased in Cape May County, New Jersey, in 1899. By 1906 over 800 people had moved into the town, which was named Whitesboro. In 1905 White left Washington for Philadelphia, resumed his law practice, and opened the People's Savings Bank, designed to help black home buyers and entrepreneurs. He also worked with the NAACP, the Frederick Douglass Hospital and other black institutions and organizations. Declining health forced White to close his bank before his death in Philadelphia on December 28, 1918.

For further reading:

Katz, William. "George H. White: A Militant Negro Congressman in the Age of Booker T. Washington." *Negro History Bulletin* 29 (March 1966): pp. 125–126.

Reid, George W. "A Biography of George H. White, 1852–1918." Ph.D. dissertation, Johns Hopkins University, 1974.

ANDREW JACKSON YOUNG, Jr.

(Moorland-Spingarn Research Center, Howard University)

United States Representative
Democrat of Georgia
Ninety-third—Ninety-fifth Congresses

On January 3, 1973, Andrew Young became the first black person to represent Georgia in Congress since Jefferson Long a century before. Young was born in New Orleans on March 12, 1932. He attended the public schools of New Orleans and graduated from the Gilbert Academy in 1947. He attended Dillard University and received a B.A. from Howard University in 1951. He attended Hartford Theological Seminary, where he received a Bachelor of Divinity in 1955. Ordained by the United Church of Christ, he served as pastor in Marion, Alabama, and in Thomasville and Beachton, Georgia. From 1957 to 1961 he was associate director of the National Council of Churches' department of youth work. In 1964 Dr. Martin Luther King, Jr., appointed Young director of the Southern Christian Leadership Conference. Young was elected executive vice president of the S.C.L.C.

in 1967. Throughout the 1960s, he helped plan S.C.L.C. campaigns to desegregate southern cities, directed training programs to assist local black leaders' preparations to hold public office and met with white business and political leaders to develop desegregation plans for their communities. From 1970 to 1972 he was chairman of the Atlanta Human Relations Commission. In 1970 he ran for Congress from the Fifth District of Georgia but lost to incumbent Republican Representative Fletcher Thompson. He won the same seat in 1972 by defeating the Republican nominee, Rodney M. Cook.

After Young entered the Ninety-third Congress he became a member of the Committee on Banking and Currency. Following his reelection in 1974 he became the first black representative to join the Committee on Rules. In January 1974, Young joined five other representatives in asking the Federal Trade Commission to suspend deceptive advertising by oil companies and public utilities and force the firms to substantiate their claims that they were working to alleviate shortages and high prices. As a congressman from a state involved in strip-mining, he gave his support to strip mining control legislation and co-sponsored an amendment blocking mining on mountain slopes exceeding twenty degrees. Taking note of the Watergate scandal, Young favored 1974 legislation limiting contributions to and spending on federal election campaigns.

Throughout his congressional career Young advocated better United States relations with and understanding of black Africa. He favored a July 1973 amendment to a foreign military aid bill requiring the President to inform Congress if Portugal used assistance to interfere in the internal affairs of its former colonies. In June 1974 Young supported legislation offered by Representative Parren Mitchell to terminate South Africa's sugar quota, contending that both white and black reformers within the country would be encouraged by United States willingness to impose economic sanctions to bring about social change. He also called on the Ford administration to refrain from recognizing Transkei, a former tribal homeland declared independent by South Africa. Young voted for the January 1975 House resolution halting $20 million in covert aid to two of the three groups fighting Angola's civil war. He asked the Senate Foreign Relations Committee to disapprove the nomination of Nathaniel Davis for assistant secretary of state for African affairs, charging that Davis, whose nomination was opposed by the foreign ministers of forty-three African countries, had been involved in covert political destabilization programs in Latin America. (Davis was confirmed but resigned several months later to accept an ambassadorial post.)

In December 1974 Young spoke out against an amendment to prohibit the Department of Health, Education and Welfare, from enforcing federal anti-discrimination laws by withholding funds from school districts that failed to comply. Recalling his work with the S.C.L.C., he supported a $125 million appropriation for an emergency school aid act to help local community school districts formulate their own desegregation plans for review by the courts. He called for extension of the Voting Rights Act of 1965 for ten years, describing improvements made in the number of black registered voters and elected officials in the South. During the 1976 presidential campaign, Young was one of Jimmy Carter's chief supporters in the black community and delivered one of the two seconding speeches for Carter at the Democratic convention.

Young resigned from Congress on January 29, 1977, to accept appointment from President Carter as United States Representative to the United Nations. He resigned as ambassador in September 1979. In April 1981 Young announced his candidacy for mayor of Atlanta. After his election in October, he assumed office on January 4, 1982, and was reelected to a second term in 1985.

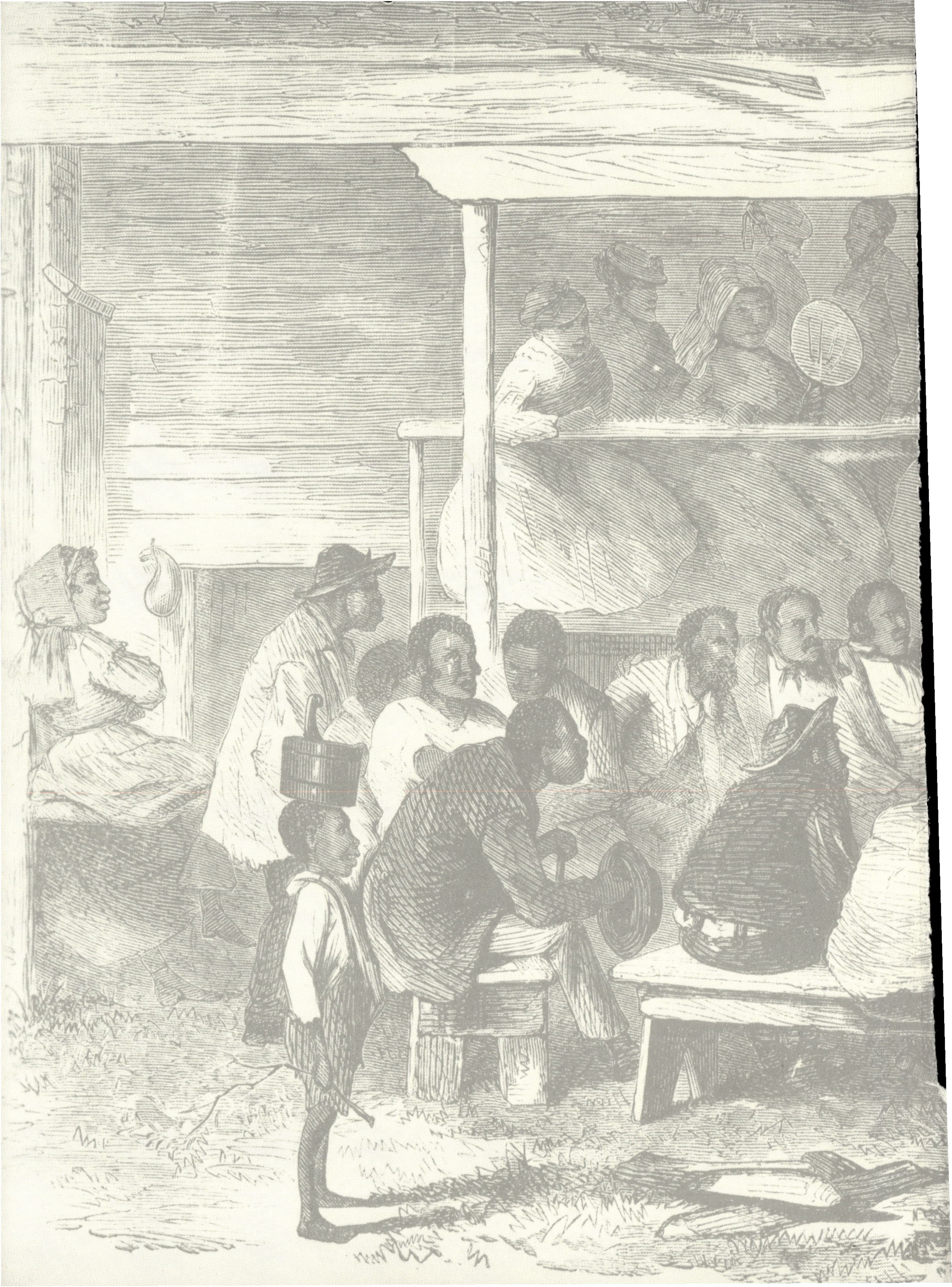